By Joe Scarborough

*The Right Path: From Ike to Reagan, How Republicans
Once Mastered Politics—and Can Again*

*The Last Best Hope: Restoring Conservatism
and America's Promise*

*Rome Wasn't Burnt in a Day: The Real Deal on How Politicians,
Bureaucrats, and Other Washington Barbarians Are
Bankrupting America*

The Right Path

THE RIGHT PATH

*From Ike to Reagan, How Republicans Once
Mastered Politics—and Can Again*

Joe Scarborough

Random House
New York

Published in the United States by Random House, an imprint of
The Random House Publishing Group, a division of Random House LLC,
a Penguin Random House Company, New York.

RANDOM HOUSE and the HOUSE colophon are
registered trademarks of Random House LLC.

Grateful acknowledgment is made to the following for permission to reprint
previously published material:

BARRY M. GOLDWATER, JR.: Excerpt from *The Conscience of a Conservative* by
Barry Goldwater. Reprinted by permission of Barry M. Goldwater, Jr.

HARPER'S MAGAZINE: Excerpt from "The Paranoid Style in American Politics"
by Richard Hofstadter, copyright © 1964 by *Harper's Magazine*. All rights
reserved. Reproduced from the November issue by special permission.

THE RONALD REAGAN PRESIDENTIAL FOUNDATION: Excerpts from two
speeches by Ronald Reagan: "A Time for Choosing" (1964) and a 1980
speech given at Liberty State Park. Courtesy of the Ronald Reagan
Presidential Foundation.

TIME MAGAZINE: Excerpt from "The Rocky Roll" from the October 6, 1958,
issue of *Time Magazine*; excerpt from "Ronald Reagan: Yankee Doodle
Magic" by Lance Morrow from the July 7, 1986, issue of *Time Magazine*. Used
by permission of *Time Magazine*.

LIBRARY OF CONGRESS CATALOGING-IN-PUBLICATION DATA
Scarborough, Joe.
The right path : from Ike to Reagan, how Republicans once
mastered politics—and can again / Joe Scarborough.
pages cm
Includes bibliographical references.
ISBN 978-0-8129-9614-2
eBook ISBN 978-0-8129-9615-9
1. Republican Party (U.S. : 1854–)—History. 2. Presidents—
United States—History. 3. United States—Politics and government. I. Title.
JK2356.S29 2013
324.2734—dc23
2013029788

Printed in the United States of America on acid-free paper

www.atrandom.com

2 4 6 8 9 7 5 3 1

First Edition

Book design by Virginia Norey

To Kate, Jack, Joey, and Andrew

Contents

Foreword

"It was invisible, as always.... On election day America is Republican until five or six in the evening. It is in the last few hours of the day that working people and their families vote, on the way home from work, or after supper; it is then, at evening, that America goes Democratic if it goes Democratic at all. All of this is invisible, for it is the essence of the act that as it happens it is a mystery in which millions of people fit one fragment of the total secret together, none of them knowing the shape of the whole."
—*Theodore H. White*, The Making of the President 1960

IN THEODORE WHITE'S NOW CANONICAL TELLING OF THE legend, the sacred democratic ritual begins as silently as snow falling on a serene New England landscape. His beautiful rendering of America's political system offers a comforting image of a peaceful process that reveals itself to a citizenry that rises the morning after an election to gaze wondrously upon the glorious results of their efforts, like watchful children awakening to winter's first snowfall. The beauty of the voting booth, seen through the lens of Teddy White's inspiring works, is how our glorious Republic moves forward.

Except when it doesn't. In those moments when a cultural shift is so sharp and sudden that its impact jars the political class out of a deep slumber, there is nothing gentle, nothing amiable about politics. These moments are more Norman Lear than Norman Rockwell, and the aftershocks seem all the more violent because few ever see a great political unraveling coming until after a Washington coalition crumbles and consensus disintegrates into cacophony.

This book tells the story of the unexpected rise and self-inflicted fall of the modern Republican Party, a movement that found a path to power in the middle of the 1960s and went on to dominate American life for forty years. With the national Grand Old Party seemingly on a glide path to ideological and demographic irrelevance as a presidential force, it's difficult to remember, but we used to be the ones to beat. From 1968 to 2008, Republicans lost only when Democrats took care to sound more conservative than liberal. Between Richard Nixon and Barack Obama, the only Democrats to win the presidency of the United States were two white Southern Baptists who sought office by positioning themselves as nontraditional Democrats who understood the failings of liberalism and appreciated the virtues of conservatism. Republicans were not beyond the mainstream of American politics. For that forty-year period, Republicans *were* the mainstream of American politics.

But as conservatives endure two terms of Barack Obama and face the possibility of eight more years with a Clinton in the White House, all too often these days it's the Republicans who sound angry, extreme, and too out of touch. If the GOP wants to regain its place as the decisive force in national politics, it needs to reengage with its real legacy, which is one of principled conservatism combined with clear-eyed pragmatism. We Republicans have been at our best when we are true to one of the deepest insights of conservatism: that politics, like mankind itself, isn't perfectible in a fallen universe. And if we continue to let the perfect become the enemy of the good, then we will continue to dwindle in influence.

The good news is that the GOP's ongoing decline as a national party is not inevitable. History tells us, actually, that we're pretty good when the odds are the longest. Republicans emerged from what seemed an invincibly liberal political culture in the middle of what *Time* founder Henry Luce called the American Century when Lionel Trilling suggested that "in the United States at this time liberalism is not only the dominant but even the sole intellectual tradition." Trilling, one of America's foremost mid-century literary critics, dismissed conservative thought as little more than "irritable mental gestures which seek to resemble ideas." History proved Trilling's quote to be as untimely as the one uttered by a British record executive who told the Beatles' manager, Brian Epstein, that bands with guitars were on their way out.

Conservatism would ultimately rise, not through "irritable mental gestures" or by being nativist or racist or blindly ideological. No, the party succeeded in direct proportion to its respect for overarching ideas about the nation and about the world that had a practical impact on the lives of Americans. Dwight Eisenhower and Ronald Reagan dominated the ideological middle of American thought because these GOP giants won elections by putting principled pragmatism ahead of reflexive purity.

Note that I say *principled* pragmatism: like our greatest leaders of any stripe—Washington, Jefferson, Jackson, Lincoln, TR, FDR, JFK—Republicans of the modern era, driven by conservatives, resonated with a majority of Americans when they demonstrated a genuine commitment to the ideas of greater liberty, a restrained state, social order, and strength abroad. These are the key conservative principles that most Americans agree with, have always agreed with, and will agree with in the future. Republicans who try to use the power of the state to interfere in matters of personal liberty will be as doomed as the big-government Democrats who wanted to use the authority of government to impose a singular "Great Society" on all of America. Conservatives know that the world is made up of what Edmund Burke described as "little platoons"—the small towns or the city neighborhoods where happiness is pursued.

The right path to power lies in appreciating that politics isn't a science but an art—that America has been at her best and will be again when the common wisdom of the people, carefully weighed in the Madisonian scales of the Constitution, has a prime place in the governance of the nation. And history shows that the common wisdom of the people is essentially conservative in that most people want to find the right balance between freedom and responsibility.

For Eisenhower and Reagan, the two great leaders of the modern Republican Party, restraint both at home and abroad were the philosophical foundations of their presidencies. Both saw their first challenge as limiting the federal government's ever-expanding reach at home. Ike's presidency followed twenty years of New Deal activism, while Reagan's focus was on reversing the more destructive, unintended consequences of LBJ's Great Society. These two Republicans won four landslide victories between them because they were also shrewd enough to yield to immovable political realities that even their landslide victories could not wash away.

General Eisenhower knew that President Eisenhower would have to employ the same principled pragmatism in the White House that served him so well as the Atlantic commander in World War II managing mercurial generals like George Patton and Bernard

Montgomery. Unlike most GOP activists in 1952, Eisenhower knew that no conservative president—no matter his popularity—would be able to eliminate Social Security and a bevy of other popular New Deal programs. It was a political pragmatism that frustrated conservatives like William F. Buckley, Jr., but it was a shrewd approach embraced even by the likes of Margaret Thatcher three decades later during her conservative revolution in the Britain of the late 1970s and 1980s. Though Thatcher remained in a perpetual political war with powerful union leaders and a socialist zeal that had laid waste to England's economy over a generation, the Iron Lady also knew that Great Britain's government-run National Health Service was simply beyond her political reach. So instead of dying a noble political death before even getting elected, Thatcher instead became the longest-serving prime minister of the twentieth century. As General George Washington learned on Long Island in the momentous summer of 1776, it is sometimes the battles great generals avoid that lead to glorious victories for freedom.

Reagan followed another GOP giant's mantra—Teddy Roosevelt's—by believing America was served best by a commander in chief who spoke softly and carried the big stick of American economic and military might. Eisenhower the general and Reagan the "warmonger" ended up being the most successful GOP politicians in the party's 160-year history while, ironically, presiding over a combined sixteen years that were among the most peaceful in the last American Century. Ike's restrained foreign policy was underscored in his farewell address to the nation as the world's greatest general ominously warned of a burgeoning "military-industrial complex."

Ike was the first Republican to run the Oval Office in two decades and held on to the White House for eight years—crushing all political comers. Reagan proved his critics wrong by being pragmatic enough to hold on to his conservative base while appealing to enough Democrats and independents to win forty-nine states in 1984. He managed that improbable feat after raising taxes, taking on Social Security, avoiding abortion battles, and allowing the federal deficit to explode to unprecedented heights. There would be compromises and deal cutting, dreams deferred and half measures accepted. The greatest conservative icon of the twentieth century knew that mortals must confront the world as it is, not as we wish it to be, if we want to win elections and bring that world closer to our ideal conservative vision.

Politics and governing aren't for the stupid or the fainthearted. And sustained conservative gains are made when candidates focus less on indulging every whim of their political base and more on what successful Republicans from Eisenhower to Nixon to Reagan focused on: bending the world to overarching conservative purposes rather than obsessing on the twists and turns of any given moment, a scenario all too sadly familiar today.

In this constitutional republic of ours, destiny belongs to leaders who speak out not only against their opponents but who also have the nerve to stand down their most ferocious supporters when the action those supporters crave would clearly prove politically disastrous. That's one of the best-kept secrets of successful statecraft, a secret that largely eluded Democrats in the years between 1968 and 1992, when presidential candidates and party operatives feared staring down the most extreme in their midst. As a result of the Democratic Party's reluctance to face down its own political extremists, the Republican Party became a moderating force to the Democrats'

extreme brand of liberalism, gained control of the contours of political debate, redesigned foreign policy, and reshaped the Supreme
Court. To understand the earth-shifting nature of just this last
change, consider this: William Rehnquist would, over this time,
move from being called the "Lone Dissenter" to "Mr. Chief Justice."

The last two decades have been less kind to the GOP. While the
right made great gains on talk radio, the Internet, and cable TV,
the party has experienced a precipitous fall in national elections. The
Republican Party's nominee has now lost the popular vote against
Democratic candidates in five of the last six presidential races. This
180-degree turn from the twenty years preceding Bill Clinton's election means the GOP's continued march toward obsolescence as a
presidential party could cost them more than the White House. It
will also tilt a closely divided Supreme Court left on issues like guns,
abortion, health care, and federalism. Those who would move the
party so far right on social issues that their nominated candidates
become unelectable are, to borrow an infamous phrase from the
Vietnam War, "destroying the village to save it."

For Republicans—and I remain a proudly defiant one—the way
forward begins with a look back. To win the future requires us, in
Lincoln's formulation, to think anew and act anew, but only after we
take a deep breath and truly come to terms with how we reached the
mountaintop and why we lost our footing. Once we do that, we shall,
God willing, save our party—and our country. This much is clear:
both need saving. There is nothing invisible or mysterious about
that.

Introduction

Forty Augusts: From Watts to Katrina

AMERICANS THINK OF AUGUST AS A TIME FOR BASEBALL AND days at the beach; for barbecues, long weekends, and back-to-school shopping. But our idyllic vision of the eighth month is divorced from the violence of history, for history tends to take big jumps in the seemingly slow days of summer. Archduke Franz Ferdinand was assassinated in Sarajevo, igniting the First World War, in August. Hiroshima and Nagasaki were obliterated in seconds as August ushered in the horrors of the atomic age. From the mobilization of the Wehrmacht to launch Case White, Hitler's invasion of Poland, to the resignation of Richard Nixon; from the nighttime escape of George Washington's army after the Battle of Long Island in 1776 to Saddam Hussein's invasion of Kuwait in 1991, August has often been the most momentous of months.

It's fitting, then, that we can trace the rise and the fall of the modern Republican Party's dominance in American politics to two Augusts forty years apart: the first in 1965, at the high-water mark of Great Society liberalism, the second in 2005, only ten months after the reelection of a Republican president led prominent GOP leaders to wonder aloud about the possibilities of a permanent Republican majority.

* * *

On Friday, August 6, 1965, the Voting Rights Act was passed into law, assuring people of color full access to the voting booth a hundred years after the chains of slavery had been broken by Lincoln. The act's passage ended the most remarkable run of legislation in U.S. history, a panoply of initiatives dubbed the Great Society, with President Lyndon B. Johnson pushing through Medicare, Medicaid, Head Start, the Civil Rights Act of 1964, and more landmark legislation in a shorter period than any previous president.

It helped that LBJ carried a martyr's cause. A year after John F. Kennedy's assassination, his vice president was swept into office with 61 percent of the popular vote, carrying 486 of 538 electoral votes in the biggest landslide since FDR swept Republican Alf Landon of Kansas aside in 1936. By the time he passed the Voting Rights Act, Johnson was carrying a 75 percent approval rating and had all but rendered helpless any Republican who dared to oppose him.

America seemed to be awash in unprecedented prosperity and the news coming out of Vietnam was so distant that the brash Texan felt comfortable using a Christmas ceremony to declare that the days of his remarkable ascent were "the most hopeful times in all the years since Christ was born in Bethlehem."

By the summer of 1965, most Americans seemed to accept that what was being built out of Washington would guarantee world peace, prosperity, even the end of disease. As it was in the years immediately following World War II, the consensus in Washington was that liberalism's ascent was all but unstoppable. LBJ was burning with confidence, perhaps because he had spent his first full year in the White House doing what George Washington, Abraham Lincoln, Franklin Roosevelt, and thirty-five previous presidents over two centuries had not been able to do: deliver on the American promise that under the law, all men were created equal. In that year, LBJ bent history without breaking a sweat. And on August 6, when Lyndon Johnson signed the Voting Rights Act, he enjoyed a level of power and popularity rarely experienced by any American president.

To the wise men of Washington, the ruthless Texan was not only driving a stake through the heart of segregation; he was also delivering a fatal blow to the two-party system itself. That August, newspaper columnists and television anchors had every reason to believe they were witnessing nothing less than the historic end of the Republican Party. The Goldwater experiment had collapsed in failure the year before, when that conservative candidate was crushed by Johnson in his historic landslide. Conservatism's intellectual force was reduced to questioning the legitimacy of national polls reaffirming LBJ's supremacy, while the party was bitterly divided between Barry Goldwater's conservative wing and Nelson Rockefeller's liberal Republican East Coast elites.

As it approached the 1966 midterms, the GOP was in such a sorry state that it could barely afford the rent to keep its national headquarters open. On the night Johnson signed the Voting Rights Act, it seemed as if the century-old duopoly that Democrats and Republicans held over American politics was coming to an end, with the Grand Old Party going the way of the Whigs.

Five days later in Los Angeles, on August 11, a white police officer pushed a black woman. That single act would start a chain reaction that would lead to the most destructive riot in U.S. history, bring down the Johnson presidency, fuel the rise of Ronald Reagan, and usher in forty years of conservatism. The fact that political and intellectual elites would fail to grasp the cultural and electoral impact of those events until the election of Reagan as California governor fourteen months later illustrates how long conventional wisdom in Washington and New York has been disconnected from the events and attitudes that shape American elections.

California voters were set on edge in the summer of 1965 by the violent Watts riots and the chaotic campus protests in Berkeley. Images of affluent white students turning over police cars and occupying administration buildings stirred resentment among middle-class voters. Images of black youths running through the burning streets of South Central Los Angeles stirred up fear among suburban whites. That fear and resentment soon turned into voter rage against a popular but disconnected California governor who spent the first days of the Watts riots on vacation in Greece. The political class's disconnect from working-class voters only fed into the cause of an aging actor who once considered himself an FDR Democrat. When he ran for governor, Ronald Reagan was dismissed by Democrats and the national media as a lightweight who harbored extreme views. His Democratic opponent, California's legendary governor Edmund "Pat" Brown, thought so little of Reagan that his allies were instructed to aid Reagan in the GOP primary.

Brown got his wish and became the first of many who aided Reagan's ascent by underestimating that remarkable politician. With the cultural chaos of 1965 erupting across the nation—Watts, Berkeley, the sexual revolution, and a growing drug culture—Reagan was a candidate who seemed born for his times. The morning after Reagan's first victory, the political elite of California and Washington awoke to observe a radical new landscape that looked nothing like the opening pages of Theodore White's *The Making of the President 1960.* Six years after JFK's win, and just two years after LBJ's historic victory had defined Goldwater conservatism as dangerously radical, it was the liberal Democratic Party that was now seen by middle-class voters as out of touch and extreme.

Two years later, the radicalism and seismic violence of the 1968 Chicago Democratic National Convention propelled Richard Nixon into the White House by the narrowest of margins and set American liberalism back on its heels for a generation. In 1980, Reagan brought his conservative revolution to Washington and finished the careers of most of the Senate's great liberal icons. Reagan followed up four years later with the historic forty-nine-state victory in 1984 and his vice president, George H. W. Bush, easily disposed of Michael Dukakis in 1988. Over the two decades following Watts and Berkeley, Republicans won five of six presidential elections by running against organized labor, Hollywood, civil rights groups, trial lawyers, and national media outlets.

But conservatives didn't need *The New York Times* or the Teamsters on their side so long as middle-class voters kept their focus set on the cultural chaos still emblematized by Watts, the Pill, Berkeley, the murders of Martin Luther King and Robert Kennedy, the violence of the Chicago convention, the Weathermen, antiwar radicalism, LSD, Woodstock, Jane Fonda, Kent State, the Black Panthers, and a multitude of radical forces that terrified voters and clung to national Democratic candidates for a generation.

In 1988, the success of George H. W. Bush's presidential campaign suggested that a right-wing pose could even elect a moderate Republican to the White House, for Bush overcame Michael Dukakis's national lead in the polls only after going to war against the

Massachusetts governor as an extremist liberal far outside the American mainstream. Yet Dukakis *was* far outside the American mainstream, and nobody who knew anything about George Bush of Andover, Yale, and Kennebunkport ever truly believed that the man his family still calls "Poppy" was simply an L.L. Bean version of George Wallace. It's a misreading of the '88 campaign to think that Republicans have to go hard-right to win. That analysis has been packaged and promulgated by frustrated liberals who want to believe that Bush won by coded racial appeals and raw red-meat patriotism. Here's the problem: furloughing first-degree murderers *isn't* a good idea, and most Americans want their children in classrooms reciting the Pledge of Allegiance.

But political winds often shift suddenly and without warning. Over the next two presidential elections, a man derided by Republican operatives as a pot-smoking, draft-dodging serial adulterer would crush two Republican heroes of World War II in presidential elections and win states in every region of the country—including the Deep South. The cultural battles that carried George H. W. Bush to victory in 1988 also propelled the GOP to a House majority for the first time in a generation, but carried no weight in presidential campaigns. Clinton, the pro-choice politician dismissed as a 1960s radical, carried states like Arkansas, Louisiana, Missouri, Tennessee, Kentucky, Georgia, and Florida. Republicans, meanwhile, were put on the defensive by a Southern strategy that failed to win the South while simultaneously managing to offend swing voters in other regions.

Before Bill Clinton's 1992 victory, Republican presidential candidates carried the state of Maine in 1972, 1976, 1980, 1984, and 1988. They also carried Connecticut in every presidential race over that same period. But in 1992, Democrats would begin a run in Maine and Connecticut that continues today. In fact, over the past two decades, the Grand Old Party's record in New England presidential contests is one win and thirty-five losses. Add New York, Pennsylvania, and New Jersey to that tally over that same time period and the party's record falls to one win and fifty-three losses. After considering that the Republican Party's record in those three big industrial states in the 1970s and 1980s was twelve wins to three losses, one can begin to see just how massive the party's falloff has been in the Northeast.

Twenty years after the '88 race, not a single New England voter was represented by a Republican in the House of Representatives. The Republican Party that had enjoyed forty-nine-state landslides over a twelve-year period is now reduced to a regional party that has carried only one New England state in two decades of presidential races. The candidate who did that, George W. Bush, was elected president in 2000 because of New Hampshire's three electoral votes, but that victory owed more to his opponent's weaknesses than the GOP's strengths. Al Gore turned in three of the worst debate performances in modern political history and decided, for reasons still unknown even to close allies, to distance himself from Bill Clinton.

The attacks of September 11 would lead to GOP victories in the 2002 off-year elections and Bush's win over John Kerry in 2004. But those wins had as much to do with America's struggle against al Qaeda as Winston Churchill's selection as prime minister in 1940 had to do with World War II. And just as Britain's six-year struggle with Nazism led exhausted voters to throw Churchill out of 10

Downing Street once victory was at hand, George W. Bush's Republican Party lost Congress when the threat of al Qaeda was less imminent. But while Churchill's leadership from 1940 to 1945 is rightfully considered one of the finest hours for any leader in recorded history, Republican stewardship of the events following the September 11 attacks on America were so poorly executed that William F. Buckley—who a half century earlier had given voice to the principles of modern conservatism and proven Lionel Trilling to be embarrassingly off base—wondered in a 2007 *National Review* column whether the Republican Party would survive the political fallout of the Iraq War.

Republicans had been winning elections for a generation after the riots and student protests of the 1960s as the party of order. The bungled war against Saddam Hussein's Iraq was just the latest in a series of cataclysmic political events that had undermined the GOP's image as the tonic to cultural chaos. From a Republican-engineered government shutdown in 1995, to the failed impeachment of a Democratic president in 1999, to Bush's divisive victory in the recount of 2000, to al Qaeda's attacks in 2001, to the Enron scandal in 2002, to the Iraq invasion in 2003 and Abu Ghraib in 2004, the political party that had promised to bring order to America's political system during the tumult of the 1960s and 1970s was viewed (often unfairly) as the creator of chaos three decades later.

The end of the GOP's forty-year reign came with the landfall of Hurricane Katrina in August 2005. Forty Augusts after riots ripped through minority neighborhoods in South Central Los Angeles, levees began to break, almost instantly submerging New Orleans's Ninth Ward.

Now Americans again saw images of black Americans on their

television sets around the clock. But forty years after images of black men rioting in the streets turned voters against liberal Democratic candidates, images of the daily suffering in New Orleans would end George W. Bush's effectiveness as a president and bring to an end the forty-year period of conservative dominance in American politics. Even George F. Will, the poet-pundit of the rise of Reaganism, detected that the administration's failures were of more than passing significance. Katrina reminded us, Will wrote in *Newsweek* in the aftermath of the storm, that conservatives must always hold that "the first business of government, on which everything depends, is security."

When government fails at such a moment, the governed have a right to wonder whether those who hold ultimate power are up to the task. The government of George W. Bush was self-evidently not. In the days and weeks following the landfall of Hurricane Katrina, my family and I made daily trips to the impacted areas in Mississippi and Louisiana. We organized the relief efforts through local churches, whose members had provided George W. Bush an overwhelming majority of their votes. But as we spent those first few weeks spreading our relief efforts across the Gulf Coast, most of those evangelical church members who were answering God's call to feed the hungry and clothe the poor began asking aloud where FEMA and other federal agencies funded by our tax dollars were. By the second week of our relief efforts, I began to notice the "Bush for President" bumper stickers from the 2004 race begin to get peeled off the minivans.

Hurricane Katrina did not turn my Southern evangelical friends into die-hard Democrats, but Katrina and Iraq did depress the GOP base and feed into a disillusionment with swing voters that led to

Nancy Pelosi being elected speaker of the House fourteen months after the hurricane came onshore. Perhaps that is because the second President Bush presided over a large, even expanding federal establishment, and yet Washington—so intent on building nations in the far corners of the earth—failed to protect the nation at home. And so in another August a world, and a biblical forty years, away from Watts, the party that found the means to rise by promising to bring order to chaos allowed chaos to trump order as an American city drowned.

This book is my effort to explain what happened in the forty Augusts between Watts and Katrina, how decisions made by Republican leaders over the past decade continue to cloud our party's future prospects, and how conservatives can in fact hold on to their base while at the same time reconnecting with those Americans who once saw the Republican Party as their best chance to move their family upward, straight into the heart of the American Dream. I do not believe that will happen. I *know* that will happen. In the pages that follow, I will tell you why.

THE RIGHT PATH

1

A Dislike for Ike

"Should any political party attempt to abolish social security and eliminate labor laws and farm programs, you
would not hear of that party again in our political history."
—*Dwight D. Eisenhower*

"It stands athwart history, yelling Stop, at a time when no
one is inclined to do so, or to have much patience with
those who do."
—*William F. Buckley, Jr.,*
in the inaugural issue of National Review,
describing the mission of the magazine

IN THE AUTUMN OF 1951, THE WHITE HOUSE WAS UNDERGO-
ing such extensive renovations—the first significant work to be done
on the house in years—that Bess and Harry Truman had moved out,
taking up residence across Pennsylvania Avenue at Blair House, the
government's guest quarters that had once been the home of Francis
Preston Blair, Andrew Jackson's confidential adviser. There President Truman sat down with General Dwight D. Eisenhower, then
supreme commander of NATO forces in Europe, who was in Washington on official business.

Over lunch on this autumn Monday—it was November 5, almost precisely a year to the day before the '52 election—the commander in chief had an offer for the visiting military hero. Should Eisenhower—the architect of Normandy, liberator of Western Europe—want it, Truman would "guarantee" the general the Democratic presidential nomination in 1952. Truman himself would step aside and vigorously campaign for the immensely popular Ike. It was not the first time Eisenhower had been approached with such a scenario. At Potsdam in 1945, shortly after Franklin Roosevelt's death had catapulted Truman into the Oval Office, the new president had told Eisenhower, "General, there is nothing you may want that I won't try to help you get. That definitely and specifically includes the presidency in 1948." Eisenhower had essentially waved Truman off, saying, "Mr. President, I don't know who will be your opponent for the presidency, but it will not be I."

Now, a presidential cycle later, Truman was back, apparently hoping an Eisenhower campaign on the Democratic ticket would extend the party's run well into the 1950s. At Blair House, however, Eisenhower again objected—but in different terms than he had at Potsdam.

"You can't join a party just to run for office," Eisenhower told Truman. In the privacy of the conversation with the president, Eisenhower said that he was not a Democrat but a Republican, and had been "all my life." For Ike, running for president still seemed out of the question, but running as a Democrat was *totally* out of the question.

Ike's protest raises an intriguing question all these years later: what did a man like Dwight Eisenhower mean when he declared himself to have been a Republican "all my life"? To be a Democrat in the Age of FDR obviously suggested support for New Deal programs and Roosevelt's foreign policy. Though divided by disagreements over the scope of government, the Democrats were largely united by a sense that the state almost always had a significant national role to play. Roosevelt's hold over Washington was the strongest of any president in U.S. history. From March of 1933 until his death a dozen springs later, FDR unleashed a blizzard of federal programs involving public works, Social Security, heavy spending, direct relief, farm aid, regulation of industry, banking restrictions, and a variety of new taxes that offended laissez-faire men all across America who shared Ike's instinctive distrust of federal interference in free markets.

The nature of the pre-1950s Republicans is more elusive. While Democrats essentially agreed that government was at least a necessary evil, many Republicans who had come of age in the dozen years of GOP dominance from 1920 to 1932 were more likely to believe government was simply an evil. In 1934, a year into the New Deal, Republican senator Robert A. Taft of Ohio said this: "The measures undertaken by the Democratic Administration are alarming. Whatever may be said for them as emergency measures, their permanent incorporation into our system would practically abandon the whole theory of American government, and inaugurate in fact socialism." The GOP in the FDR years was a coalition of free-enterprisers and protectionists as well as internationalists (largely in the East) and isolationists (largely in the Midwest). The GOP that languished in the minority under Roosevelt's expansive vision of government was the ideological child of the 1920s president Calvin Coolidge, a leader who refused to provide federal aid to depressed farmers or check the more extreme economic elements of the Roaring Twenties. But the

Grand Old Party dominated American politics in the years leading up to the Great Depression because, as the influential columnist Walter Lippmann observed in 1926, Coolidge Republicans had a talent for effectively doing nothing: "This active inactivity suits the mood and certain of the needs of the country admirably. It suits all the business interests which want to be let alone. . . . And it suits all those who have become convinced that government in this country has become dangerously complicated and top-heavy." In other words there's always been an antigovernment strain in American politics that waxes and wanes. It waxed in the 1920s and waned under FDR.

There were, of course, gradations of conviction and of intensity within the GOP. Eisenhower held more pragmatic views on economic and foreign policy than those advanced by Coolidge's cool and aloof policies or Taft's red-hot rhetoric. For a man like Eisenhower, Republicanism at home meant a belief in the power of free markets and the promotion of fiscal responsibility. Abroad, the Kansas soldier naturally belonged to the party's more internationalist wing. As a military man he understood the importance of America's involvement in the world, even though he was extremely cautious as president about the application of U.S. power.

Eisenhower was, in other words, part of the mainstream of the GOP of the 1930s and 1940s. After declining Truman's offer of the Democratic presidential nomination, Ike publicly announced himself to be a Republican when he finally decided to seek the presidency in early 1952. After a heated primary struggle against Robert Taft, Eisenhower stormed to victory against Adlai Stevenson after twenty years of Democratic dominance. Ike would easily win the White House in two landslide victories under the GOP banner.

* * *

Despite returning Republicans to power after two aimless decades in the political wilderness, no Republican during his time was more resented within his own party than Dwight Eisenhower. William A. Rusher, the publisher of *National Review*, said "modern American conservatism largely organized itself during, and in explicit opposition to, the Eisenhower Administration." And William F. Buckley's 1955 declaration that *National Review* should stand athwart history yelling "Stop" was a primal scream from the right directed as much at the Republican president as at Ike's Democratic opposition.

Why? How did Eisenhower, the man who led the Republicans back to power through the strength of his practiced charm and likability, become a source of conservative outrage? The story of Ike's relatively quick journey from GOP standard-bearer to conservative scapegoat sheds light on the current Republican Party weakness of preferring ideological purity over the kind of principled conservative pragmatism that actually wins elections.

In the early 1950s the Republicans began a gradual but unmistakable shift from being a political institution that was a pragmatic collection of various factions to being an ideological institution that would, when at its very worst, choose nominees in state and national elections who could check every box required to advance an ideological agenda except one: winning. Political institutions reflect a diversity of views and interests and tend to be given to compromise. Ideological institutions, on the other hand, seek to embody a pure creed and ignore the harsh political realities that lay before them.

Like the Democratic Party of the 1970s and 1980s, this kind of descent into ideological extremism is less damaging in congressional races than in presidential races. Ideology is dramatic and seductive—but politics is about history and people and the messiness of the world. As William Buckley himself would say long after Ike left office, "Idealism is fine, but as it approaches reality, its costs become prohibitive." Still, it's easier to mobilize people around the clarity of ideas—adherence to doctrine—than around the virtues of compromise. The tension between ideology and principled pragmatism, still so important and even decisive in Republican politics in the first quarter of the twenty-first century, has its origins in the tensions between Dwight Eisenhower and the rising conservative movement.

I'm often frustrated when I try to explain to fellow Republicans how I can both agree with the most ideological of small-government conservatives while counseling them to strike tough bargains with more moderate members if compromise is the only way to move the conservative agenda forward. Like Reagan in the 1980s, Ike knew that he could often advance the Republican cause only by making deals with the congressional Democrats who ran Capitol Hill. That kind of pragmatic position repelled a younger Bill Buckley during the Eisenhower era, but an example of Buckley adopting the same stance a decade later was when he came rushing to the defense of newly elected California governor Ronald Reagan, then under attack from the right for passing big budgets and striking deals with Democratic lawmakers in Sacramento. Buckley would openly mock Reagan's conservative critics who dared to challenge his new conservative champion, asking whether they would prefer he "padlock the state treasury and give speeches on the Liberty amendment?" (The Liberty Amendment was a right-wing favorite designed to limit the powers of the federal government drastically.)

* * *

But in the mid-1950s, Buckley, Rusher, and an emerging conservative insurgency burned with rage against the Communist threat and civil disorder. In his landmark publishing debut, *God and Man at Yale,* Buckley struck out against Yale college professors whose salaries were drawn from the contributions of "Christian individualists" while seeking to convert their sons to the cause of "atheistic socialism." Bill Buckley was fearless, attacking not only Republican presidents and liberal institutions, but also his own pope. When Pope Paul VI wrote an encyclical on world peace—an encyclical with which the more hawkish Buckley disagreed—the writer Garry Wills got a call from his devout Catholic editor. Buckley's purpose, Wills recalled, was to "check a quote from Thomas Aquinas—the dictum that Popes may err, in moral decisions, *propter falso testes* ("because of erring witnesses to points of fact").

Buckley interjected, "Doesn't testicle come from the same word as witness?"

Wills said yes, but urged the editor "to hold off on a column that would make certain Catholics angrier than ever at Buckley's magazine."

Buckley would have none of it. As Wills recalled, "I could hear his typewriter already Latinizing while his shoulder pinned the phone to his head . . . . Why not hold off a day or two?" Wills asked.

"Because I don't have *falso testes*," came the classic Buckley reply. And that was that.

The brilliant ideological combatant proclaimed his band of conservative followers the "new radicals" and he was right. Buckley's was a radicalism created out of contempt—contempt for an establishment that had spent the FDR years running over the rights of individuals, had fired General Douglas MacArthur before losing China, had allowed the Soviets to get the bomb, and had ceded Eastern Europe to Stalin while FDR's men were concocting grand designs for a new international order. While it may be difficult to pinpoint precisely when Buckley's brand of conservatism was born, faraway Yalta may have contributed as much as anything to the shaping of modern conservatism, and of modern politics.

Before the winter of 1945, the Crimea was known to Americans, if it were known at all, as the site of the nineteenth-century war that had given us Tennyson's "Charge of the Light Brigade." "Theirs not to reason why," wrote Tennyson: their duty was "to do and die." Ever since the Big Three—Franklin Roosevelt, Winston Churchill, and Joseph Stalin—gathered at Yalta for what would be FDR's final wartime conference, historians have puzzled over what happened, and why, in sessions that gave Stalin's Red Army a greater hand in Eastern Europe as the war against Hitler ground to a close. (Churchill hated the Crimea, saying, "We could not have found a worse place for a meeting if we had spent ten years on research.") Still, at the time, liberals and pro-Roosevelt forces believed a historic deal had been reached since Stalin had agreed to participate in both the war against Japan and in the proposed United Nations organization. The latter was seen as an essential tool to peacekeeping in the aftermath of this the second global war in just the first half of the twentieth century.

"We really believed in our hearts that this was the dawn of the new day we had all been praying for and talking about for so many years," Roosevelt adviser Harry Hopkins later told the playwright and FDR speechwriter Robert E. Sherwood. "We were absolutely certain that we had won the first great victory of the peace—and, by 'we,' I mean *all* of us, the whole civilized human race."

Like most flights of euphoria, the post-Yalta high was short-lived. Hopkins and Churchill were soon to wake to sobering news that Stalin had expanded the Soviet reach across the areas of Central and Eastern Europe where Russia's army had "liberated" tens of millions of Europeans from the grip of Nazi control into the hands of Soviet totalitarianism. American conservatives soon came to see the Crimean conference as a watershed moment where a Washington establishment embodied in the likes of Henry Wallace and Alger Hiss had sold out American interests on the scale of Britain's 1938 Munich Pact with Nazi Germany. The party that had offered a home to isolationists before Pearl Harbor (as did the Democrats) reacted to the deal with Stalin with ferocity, a reaction made all the more violent by the perception that Roosevelt had played the key role in appeasing the Soviet Union.

FDR was so hated in some quarters of America that people who could not bring themselves to speak his name just referred to him as "That Man." To many Republicans, the New York patrician was more than a traitor to his class; he was a traitor to American capitalism. The same president who lorded over a legislative program many considered antithetical to free enterprise was now the commander in chief who had essentially surrendered Eastern Europe to the USSR.

For conservatives, Yalta now brought together two irresistible forces: contempt for Roosevelt and the growing fear of Communism's spread. Both were potent in and of themselves. Mixed together in the story of the sellout at Yalta they fed on one another.

After five years of standing shoulder to shoulder with a Democratic president leading the fight against Adolf Hitler, Republicans suddenly had a case to make against FDR on foreign policy that was equal in weight to the domestic case against the New Deal. Roosevelt was now not only the embodiment of socialism at home. He was, because of Yalta, an abettor of Communism abroad. It may have been an oversimplification of actual events, but most powerful political arguments usually are. The linkage of an expansive government at home with a weak foreign policy abroad gave the right an internally coherent political philosophy that would grow steadily in the postwar years and eventually lead to landslide victories for both Richard Nixon and Ronald Reagan. Liberalism's failures at Yalta, in China, and in the nuclear arms race's infancy gave Buckley and his apostles the kick-start that "movement conservatism" needed. America's political system would never be the same.

You could see its potency only a year after the conference ended. In California's 12th Congressional District, east of Los Angeles, a group of Republicans calling themselves the Committee of 100 were desperate. Locked out of the White House since 1933, the district, which was evenly split between Democrats and Republicans, had been held by Democratic representative Jerry Voorhis for a decade. The GOP needed someone fresh and energetic to take the seat back and set out to interview possible nominees.

One stood out. A young Navy veteran, still in his officer's uniform, accepted an invitation to appear before the group to make the case for himself. He spoke in classically Republican terms about free enterprise, noting the two different approaches in America. "One advocated by the New Deal is government control in regulating all our lives," said Richard Nixon. "The other calls for individual freedom and all that initiative can produce. I hold with the latter viewpoint." Nixon made a generational plea as well: "I believe the returning veterans, and I have talked to many of them in the fox-holes, will not be satisfied with a dole or a government handout. They want a respectable job in private industry where they will be recognized for what they produce, or they want the opportunity to start their own business."

By mid-October, Nixon was capitalizing on Americans' fear of Communism. "REMEMBER," said a Nixon ad, "Voorhis is a former registered Socialist and his voting record in Congress is more So-cialistic and Communistic than Democratic." On the eve of the gen-eral election, there were reports of phone calls in the 12th District. When a voter would answer the phone, a voice would say: "This is a friend of yours, but I can't tell you who I am. Did you know that Jerry Voorhis is a Communist?" Nixon won with 56 percent of the vote. The ambitious vet would use such tactics to fuel a meteoric rise in Congress, one that would carry him to the United States Senate while still in his thirties.

But Richard Nixon was not alone. The 1946 midterms were hugely successful for Republicans, as history seemed to be moving away from the Democrats, only one year after FDR's death.

That is, until Americans went to the polls again two years later. In the 1948 presidential election, Harry Truman, who had been written off by everybody but the voters, pulled off one of the great political comebacks in American history, railing against the "do-nothing" 80th GOP Congress. Interestingly, then as now, Nixon's new brand of uncompromising Republicanism worked well at the local and state level but was less successful at the national one. Truman even carried Nixon's own state of California.

Harry S. Truman's stunning victory spoke to an important, and

often overlooked, trait of the American voter: that of avoiding extremes at all costs on the presidential level. The 1948 election is a
particularly good example of this, with voters having not two but
four choices. There was Truman, the New Deal Democrat; Thomas
E. Dewey, the traditional (and uninspiring) Republican; Henry A.
Wallace, the Progressive Party's ultraliberal nominee; and Strom
Thurmond, the segregationist Dixiecrat whose break with the Democrats over civil rights foreshadowed much of what was to come in
presidential politics.

Truman's come-from-behind victory delayed, but could not stop,
the growth of the Republican right. In fact, in some ways, the defeat
of Dewey, who was depicted as a creature of an Eastern establishment that seemed all too cozy with the world of New Dealers and
internationalists, stoked the right's rise. An extension of the Truman
administration gave conservatives, in Nixon's memorable phrase, a
richer target, as the reign of "Dean Acheson and his College of Cow-
ardly Containment" ran a bit longer. Congressman Nixon's victory
in the 1950 Senate race in California sent a clear signal: the electoral
future might well belong to Republicans raw enough to say, as Nixon
did of his female opponent, that she was "pink right down to her
underwear."

It was not the kind of thing Dwight Eisenhower might say.

Ever.

And yet in the summer of 1952, Eisenhower summoned Richard
Nixon to ask him to join the GOP ticket: Eisenhower the internationalist Republican with conservative domestic instincts, Nixon
the hungry young emblem of the striving postwar middle class, a

politician convinced that his best shot at the main chance in the post-Yalta world was to stoke anxieties over Communist strength abroad and infiltration at home.

To step back from the image of the ticket of Ike and Dick and see the present and future of Republican politics in its component parts is clearly right—Ike was more moderate in temperament than his younger, more ambitious running mate—but far too many observers, particularly casual ones, leave the conversation there, essentially accepting the era's conservative conventional wisdom that Eisenhower was staid, uninspiring, and centrist. To many conservatives, Eisenhower was the past, Nixon the future; moderation was yesterday's creed, conservatism tomorrow's.

The problem with this argument—as familiar as it is—is that it doesn't hold up to scrutiny. Eisenhower was in many ways the more complicated figure. He was uncomfortable with Nixon-style Red-hunting and was determined not to radically transform America's postwar economy, which had grown greatly when Washington went to war in 1941. Ike was a champion of fiscal restraint and had far more confidence in corporate CEOs than liberal bureaucrats, but Ike was not Calvin Coolidge. The general who liberated Europe from Hitler knew the continent was still reeling from a war that had killed millions of Europeans and ravaged the continent's industrial infrastructure. Stalinism was on the march and many believed that Western Europe could fall under the Soviets' control. But instead of wielding an ideological flamethrower, Ike took a more nuanced approach to America's great challenges at home and abroad. While Eisenhower refused to undermine FDR's most popular New Deal programs, he tried to balance the budget, champion free enterprise, and stem the tide of government expansion. Overseas, Eisenhower remained engaged in world affairs but was best known for the restraint he showed—forging a peace pact in Korea, keeping America's allies at arm's length during the Suez Crisis of 1956, and working tirelessly to keep U.S. troops out of combat.

Eisenhower's subtle approach may have angered conservatives who wanted to reverse what they saw as FDR radicalism, but the general knew how to most shrewdly employ his political troops and ensure that the GOP would dominate the nation's capital throughout the 1950s. Voters indeed liked Ike, who was swept to overwhelming victories in two national elections through force of character and confidence in his conviction that most Americans had made their peace with much of the New Deal, or at least with much of the Democratic vision of a more engaged government. He won because his sense of the people was more sophisticated than the emotional instincts of a young Buckley and his self-described new radicals.

Eisenhower understood something that too few leaders in American history have: that presidents are more than party men, more than ideologues, more than campaigners. Party, ideology, and the arts of campaigning all have a role to play in the orchestration of a successful presidency. But at heart Eisenhower agreed with Henry Adams, who once wrote that a president is like "the commander of a ship at sea. He must have a helm to grasp, a course to steer, a port to seek."

Commanders of ships are like generals on the battlefield. To succeed in their missions they must deal with the world—weather, geography, morale, the strength of the foe—as it is. Ignoring reality or dismissing it may be dramatic, but more often than not the guy who damns the torpedoes ends up sunk.

Eisenhower understood this political truth long before many in the rising conservative movement would. He grasped that power would come to those who talked about big things in a big, inclusive way. One of his aides, Arthur Larson, wrote a book entitled *A Republican Looks at His Party* in which he argued that "Modern Republicanism" required a middle way between the extremes of left and right—a view whose political validity throughout the 1950s was affirmed by Eisenhower's victories. While that wasn't the case in a number of off-year congressional elections, it has been the case in every modern presidential election with the exception of Reagan's 1980 win.

How is it that Eisenhower knew this when so many others—including, early on, his own running mate—did not? Part of it can be traced to the life experiences of America's greatest general. The military puts a premium on performance, on achieving a given goal. Posturing is not unknown, but many of the greatest generals in our history have been quieter men who dealt less in certitude and more in problem solving. The greatest generals, including Eisenhower, have to be astute politicians, building coalitions with reluctant allies, soothing the egos of fellow officers, and communicating vision and purpose to a broad constituency of fighting men. Eisenhower was masterly at this work, and his travels and oversight of a vast, multinational war effort gave him a deep appreciation of the significance of cultural differences—and the importance of being able to harness a diversity of views and opinions toward a common goal.

Eisenhower has long been the subject of historical revisionism. Beginning with Fred Greenstein's book *The Hidden-Hand Presidency: Eisenhower as Leader* in 1982, historians who once dismissed the thirty-fourth president as a disconnected manager, controlled by corporate interests and less interested in policy than golf, now see him as an effective executive who wielded power ruthlessly behind the scenes while directing America through eight years of unprecedented peace and prosperity.

It is now time for Republicans to embrace that assessment. Within the councils of the party, too many activists still dismiss Eisenhower as a bland moderate, a figure of safety and accommodation, even a Democrat in Republican golf cleats whose conservatism could never equal that of Nixon or Reagan or George W. Bush.

But Eisenhower, unlike recent GOP presidential nominees, knew how to win elections and how to govern conservatively. He may not have abolished Social Security or started World War III to drive Stalin out of Europe, but he contained the size and scope of government and he laid the foundations for national greatness through the construction of interstate highways and, in the wake of Sputnik in 1957, by funding science and technology education and innovation. The phrase "Eisenhower Republican" has been used derisively for too long. That is a shame. We should learn from his example.

You be the judge. Here is an Eisenhower memo, written by hand, early in his first term. He was coming to power after years of big spending, both at home and on the military. Care had to be taken, the president said, noting:

There will be an immediate & radical revision in the objectives of the fiscal policy of the Gov[ernment]. However, our economic machinery is so delicately balanced that the accomplishment of these new objectives will proceed cautiously and slowly, making progress over an extended period, taking only a short step at a time.

Like a heavy truck racing down an icy hill, the brakes must

*be lightly and expertly applied to avoid a wreck and slowly come
to a stop before turning off in the right direction.*

*The inheritance from the outgoing administration of not only
an enormous debt but plus a generally unappreciated tremendous amount of present commitments for future payments upon
past obligations further seriously complicates any rapid accomplishment of the revisions required.*

Hardly a leftist tract. But GOP activists did not care. They believed that Eisenhower failed the two central tests of the time. Put in
its rawest terms, the conservative wing did not believe that Eisenhower hated either government or Communism enough. A movement shaped by reaction to the New Deal and to Yalta did not want
the kind of leadership Eisenhower was offering. As Buckley wrote in
the inaugural issue of *National Review*, the new conservative movement wanted to stop the flow of history, not bend it gradually. Perhaps that is because the fevered atmosphere of the 1950s was in
many ways apocalyptic. The Soviets had the bomb; China had been
lost to the Communists; democracy itself seemed as much if not
more at risk than it had in the 1930s, when Stalin, Hitler, Mussolini,
and Hirohito were pursuing power. These were desperate times.

Eisenhower himself was somewhat puzzled by the contempt he
stirred in purists. Ike saw himself as consummately conservative. In
his memoirs, trying to explain his approach to domestic policy, he
quoted a 1932 speech of FDR's: "Our industrial plant is built," Roosevelt had said. "The problem just now is whether under existing
conditions it is not overbuilt. Our last frontier has long since been
reached. . . . Our task now is not discovery or exploitation of natural
resources, or necessarily producing more goods. It is the soberer,

less dramatic business of administering resources and plants already in hand . . . of distributing wealth and products more equitably."

Reflecting on the passage, Eisenhower commented: "I did not share the belief that the American economy was overbuilt; that parceling out scarcities was the way to economic justice; that the federal government had to establish a rigid economic order for the whole country; that only a Niagara of federal spending could power the country's economic progress; and that, all other things being equal, the federal government deserved first opportunity and had the right to solve any major problem that might arise in the nation."

He was practical, though, about what could be done. "In initiating a reversal of trends based on such beliefs—trends which by 1953 were twenty years old—we were setting in motion revolutionary activity," Eisenhower added. "We suffered no delusion that such a revolution could become a reality through the frenzied drama of a first one hundred days, or that it could be the work of improvisation, however clever." This last was a subtle but unmistakable shot at Roosevelt, whose haphazard White House management drove order-loving Republicans like Ike to distraction.

When it came down to it, Eisenhower was unwilling to sacrifice reality to ideology. During the 1952 campaign he had pledged to get federal spending down to what now seems to be a modest sum of $70 billion a year but found that circumstances were more complicated than he had thought. In what should sound familiar to us, Eisenhower discovered that after defense spending and "relatively uncontrollable major programs under existing legislation" (interest on debt, veterans' and farm programs, unemployment insurance) there was only a fraction of discretionary spending left over from which to cut.

He'd now need $72 billion—$2 billion more than he'd promised Senator Taft in a meeting at Morningside Heights in Manhattan during the campaign. This left a deficit (albeit a smaller one than Truman had projected). At a gathering with legislative leaders on April 30, 1953, Eisenhower informed them that "it would be impossible for us to arrive at a balanced budget immediately; a too rapid reduction in the budget, I said, would have bad repercussions both at home and abroad."

According to Eisenhower, the announcement "astounded and upset Senator Taft. This administration, he argued heatedly, was spending almost as much as the preceding one, and the result would be either more debt or more taxes, and the certain defeat of Republican candidates in 1954." Why not take on the military budgets? ("I have no confidence whatsoever in their judgment or their ability to break away from recommendations they have made in the past," Taft said of the armed services.)

Eisenhower's men noted the president's rising temper. (Behind that grin lay a volcanic capacity for anger.) They jumped in, Eisenhower recalled, which gave him "time to cool off before answering."

He could not do everything at once, Eisenhower said, and he was not going to compromise national security for tax cuts. "I wanted to see a tax reduction," Eisenhower said. "But I wanted even more to stop the deterioration of the currency which had been going on for so many years under unsound fiscal and monetary policies. And, between the Scylla of a deep deficit and the Charybdis of an inadequate military budget, we had to make a start without encountering either."

He would, in the end, balance the budget, in part because of the remarkable growth of the economy, but also because of a newfound fiscal discipline that he brought to Washington. He would also maintain our security posture while avoiding military conflict after he struck a peace deal in Korea. John F. Kennedy's later allegations about a "missile gap" between the United States and the Soviets were pure fiction. And Eisenhower would essentially ratify parts of the New Deal, expanding Social Security and maintaining a significant federal presence in the economy.

On the more emotional question of Communism, Eisenhower was certainly no McCarthy, though the president did from time to time try to have it both ways. In 1952, much to his later embarrassment, Eisenhower had failed to read a section of a speech defending fellow general George C. Marshall from McCarthy's charges of treason for fear of offending the right. In the White House he avoided direct confrontations with McCarthy, figuring that the increasingly reckless Wisconsin senator would flame out.

McCarthy did exactly this, but it took several years. "It seemed that almost every day I had to point out that if I were to attack Senator McCarthy, even though every personal instinct so prompted me, I would greatly enhance his publicity value without achieving any constructive purpose," Eisenhower recalled. By the end of the senator's season of power in Washington, in late 1954, McCarthy began accusing the president himself of Communist sympathies. No one took this very seriously, but on the far corners of the emerging right McCarthy created the impression that Eisenhower was not as devout an anticommunist as he ought to be—an impression that fueled a growing sense of grievance that, added to the sense that FDR's home front was being expanded rather than contracted, gave the purists all that much more to rail against.

* * *

Rail they did. There was *National Review* in 1955 and the founding of the Young Americans for Freedom at Buckley's parents' house in Sharon, Connecticut, five years later. There was the emergence of the ultraright John Birch Society in 1958, which held outright that Eisenhower was a Communist tool. And, tellingly, in the waning months of the Eisenhower presidency, came a small book that would have a big impact. Published in the spring of 1960, the 127-page tract had been ghostwritten by Brent Bozell, Bill Buckley's brother-in-law, for Barry Goldwater, Republican of Arizona. It was called *The Conscience of a Conservative,* and if anyone had any doubt about Goldwater's view of Eisenhower, one had only to read the first few pages of the book, which became a surprise best-seller.

The New Deal, Dean Acheson wrote approvingly in a book called A Democrat Looks at His Party, *"conceived of the federal government as the whole people organized to do what had to be done." A year later Mr. [Arthur] Larson wrote* A Republican Looks at His Party, *and made much the same claim in his book for Modern Republicans. The "underlying philosophy" of the New Republicanism, said Mr. Larson, is that "if a job has to be done to meet the needs of the people, and no one else can do it, then it is the proper function of the federal government."*

But Goldwater would have none of this, commenting:

Here we have, by prominent spokesmen of both political parties, an unqualified repudiation of the principle of limited govern-

ment. There is no reference by either of them to the Constitution, or any attempt to define the legitimate functions of government. The government can do what needs to be done; note, too, the implicit but necessary assumption that it is the government itself that determines what needs to be done. We must not, I think, underrate the importance of these statements. They . . . propound the first principle of totalitarianism: that the State is competent to do all things and is limited in what it actually does by the will of those who control the State. . . . The result is a Leviathan, a vast national authority out of touch with the people, and out of their control. The monolith of power is bounded only by the will of those who sit in high places.

It was an electrifying book for conservatives. The right now had a clear idea who it would like to catapult to the highest levels: Goldwater himself. Conservative leaders would hound the Arizona senator throughout Vice President Richard Nixon's 1960 run for president, asking Goldwater to work with them to dump Ike's vice president for conservatism's bright new star. Nixon crushed those dreams with little effort but after his narrow loss to John Kennedy, the Goldwater machine kicked into motion. And so began a four-year mission in search of ideological purity that would ultimately catapult Barry Goldwater to his party's presidential nomination.

It was an understandable urge of movement conservatives after enduring two decades of Roosevelt rule and two terms of what they considered statism by Ike. But that search for purity at the ballot box was a fatally flawed approach to presidential politics that depended more on grievance and resentment than mundane traits (such as lik-

ability) that help leaders like Ike beat their liberal Democratic opponents in such convincing fashion.

Republican candidates would share in no such good fortune in
the first half of the 1960s. Quickly forgetting the lessons of their
two-term president, the GOP would instead spend the better part of
the next decade struggling to escape complete political irrelevance.

2

Between a Rock and the Right

"I do not undertake to promote welfare, for I propose to extend freedom.... And if I should later be attacked for neglecting my constituents' 'interests,' I shall reply that I was informed their main interest is liberty and that in that cause I am doing the very best I can."

—*Barry Goldwater*, The Conscience of a Conservative

"The only answer to a strategy of victory for the Communist world is a strategy of victory for the free world. Let the victory we seek ... be the victory of freedom over tyranny, of plenty over hunger, of health over disease, in every country of the world."

—*Richard Nixon, accepting the*
1960 Republican presidential nomination

TOM DEWEY HAD SOME ADVICE FOR RICHARD NIXON. THE 1958 midterm elections were coming up and the economy was in a cyclical downturn—nothing out of the ordinary in the course of things, but downturns are always bad for the incumbent party. Eisenhower made a habit of subcontracting much of the administration's political work to his younger and more partisan vice president, and so the expectation was that Nixon would soon hit the road—the Republicans' most prominent spokesman.

Now a party wise man, Dewey advised against Nixon's becoming overly involved in '58. "I know that Ike won't do it, and I know that all those old party wheelhorses will tell you stories that will pluck your heartstrings, but you're toying with your chance to be President," Dewey told Nixon. "Don't do it, Dick. You've already done enough, and 1960 is what counts now." Dewey, a man who had lost the 1948 presidential election to Harry Truman in heartbreaking fashion, knew a thing or two about the challenges facing a Republican in a presidential campaign. He also had insight into Ike's ruthless approach toward Nixon. Dewey was, after all, Eisenhower's hatchet man in 1952 tasked to deliver the news to the young vice presidential candidate that General Eisenhower no longer wanted him on the ticket and thought it best that Nixon quietly step down.

Richard Nixon ignored Thomas Dewey's counsel in 1952 and did so again six years later. "In the end, I took on the task because it had to be done, and because there wasn't anyone else to do it," Nixon recalled long afterward. Feeling the approaching storm of Election Day, though, Nixon acknowledged that in the end "I labored under a feeling of total hopelessness."

His feelings were justified. Years later he said the results "still make me wince": the Democrats increased their Senate majority by thirteen seats and their House majority by forty-seven seats, and Republicans lost thirteen out of twenty-one gubernatorial races.

To rub it in, on the morning after the election Nixon was informed that the conventional wisdom on television was that there had been one big winner and one big loser in the midterms. The loser, of course, was Richard Nixon, whose campaigning had failed to prevent the Democratic landslide. Even worse for the vice president was the name of the winner with a familiar name but a fresh electoral political face: Nelson Rockefeller. The Empire State millionaire had defeated fellow magnate Averell Harriman for the New York governorship.

Nixon thus awoke to a political world in which the 1960 presidential election was two years away, and his two most formidable foes—Rockefeller in the East and Goldwater in the West—were two of the only Republicans nationwide who were coming off strong showings with the voters. "My campaigning had had little visible effect, had gained me little thanks or credit, and had tarred me with the brush of partisan defeat at a time when my potential rivals for the nomination, Rockefeller and Barry Goldwater, were basking in the glory of victory," Nixon gloomily recalled. "Perhaps Dewey had been right: I should have sat it out."

Too late for that, though, and now, for Nixon and for the GOP, the action shifted to the contest for the nomination to succeed Eisenhower. Shortly after the midterm disaster, Nixon adjourned for a strategy session at his friend and confidant Bebe Rebozo's place at Key Biscayne. As the vice president saw it, it was a three-way race, with Rockefeller and Goldwater presenting the greatest challenges to his own emergence from Ike's shadow as the standard-bearer.

Often the story of modern Republican politics begins with 1964 in large part because of Teddy White's influential account of the 1960 election and the well-burnished fable of John F. Kennedy himself. Yet to understand what came after, we must first look at Richard Nixon's torturous battles waged inside a party of activists who had little respect for the sitting GOP president and little use for the vice president who wanted desperately to succeed him. Nixon's story in the epic campaign of 1960 illuminates as well as any the perennial struggle within the Republican Party between ideological purity and national appeal.

If Nixon represented the striving new middle class, and if Goldwater embodied the frontier culture of individualism and independence and reinvention, Nelson Aldrich Rockefeller was the personification of the old and the established. Born into one of the wealthiest families in the world in their summer mansion in Bar Harbor, Rockefeller went to Dartmouth, married a socialite from Philadelphia's Main Line, spent summers sailing competitively in Seal Harbor, Maine, developed an interest in South America, and collected an immense amount of modern art. He also held positions in the administrations of FDR, Truman, and Eisenhower, and set his sights on the presidency from the moment he won his 1958 race for governor. Nelson once famously said, "I've never found it a handicap to be a Rockefeller." The family name and his massive wealth kept Rockefeller in the center of Republican politics until he left the office of vice president in 1977.

The October 6, 1958, issue of *Time* had a Rockefeller portrait on the cover which added yet one more grievance to Richard Nixon's growing list of complaints against a Northeast caste of elites whose acceptance he had always craved but whose rejection he had always felt. As Jeffrey Frank masterfully recounted in *Ike vs. Dick,* the young Navy vet who finished at the top of his law class at Duke first felt the sting of that rejection after being turned down for work by every Wall Street firm that interviewed him after the war. Within a few years of his congressional career, the media elite began harboring open contempt for a man they would never forgive for his tireless anticommunist crusades, and specifically, for his relentless pursuit of Alger Hiss. Hiss, a protected member of that most elite caste, was eventually proven to be a Soviet spy and sentenced to jail for five years. Even after Whittaker Chambers dramatically made Nixon's case by producing the "Pumpkin Papers" (classified documents secretly copied by Hiss), many in the media remained loyal to Hiss and focused their rage instead on Richard Nixon. So contemptuous were many in the media of RN that after his bitter defeat in the 1962 California governor's race, ABC-TV's Howard K. Smith produced a special titled *The Political Obituary of Richard Nixon*. There to comment, as a special guest, was Soviet spy and convicted perjurer Alger Hiss.

Given the brutal treatment the national media had always heaped upon the Orange County Republican, Richard Nixon should not have been surprised that *Time* ignored a sitting vice president who had spent most of 1958 doing the party's dirty work as its standard-bearer, and instead gave their valuable cover story to a fellow Northeasterner whose campaign was built on little more than a family name and fortune.

According to the magazine, the Rockefeller gubernatorial campaign came about this way:

> *Following a family tradition, Rockefeller one afternoon last winter called an unpublicized family council in the 56th-floor Rockefeller Center suite from which the Rockefellers guide their worldwide enterprises and philanthropies. To his brothers he outlined his newest intention: he was anxious to run for office; some Republicans suggested he announce for Governor. Said he: "I think I'll give it a whirl."*
>
> *Also whirling away were four other Republican hopefuls, in-*

cluding former Republican National Chairman Leonard Wood Hall, a Long Islander who had already got President Eisenhower's off-the-cuff endorsement. But not even sage Len Hall had a chance. By August, Rockefeller had collected delegates enough to turn the state Republican convention into a formality. By September, scarcely pausing for breath, he was on the campaign stump, attracting larger crowds than the most optimistic Republicans had expected. Everyone agreed Nelson Rockefeller was a political golden boy; everyone suggested a different reason why. Said brother Laurance, an amateur psychologist: "He has reached a degree of maturity really free of egotism, fears and frustrations, and is able to project himself into the problems of others." Said amiably disgruntled Leonard Hall: "He's got magic."

Conservative Republicans would forever distrust the wealthy magician's sleight of hand. In political terms, he was more than a little liberal on issues that the conservative element of the Republican Party held dear. Rockefeller was progressive on civil rights (as was Nixon, though the vice president rarely received the credit he deserved on the issue) and favored a larger government role in securing the social safety net. Rockefeller's was the kind of domestic Republicanism that the anti–New Dealers had hated for nearly thirty years now. To the right, Rockefeller was an Eastern interloper in a new political age that belonged to Southern and Western heroes. He was a government man in an antigovernment time. He was, in a way, the party's first and most famous RINO—"Republican in Name Only"—the conservative charge now leveled against any Republican who moves slightly away from orthodoxy.

Yet he was a popular and powerful figure on the national stage, and Nixon watched Rockefeller carefully and warily. The vice president was right to worry.

"I hate the thought of Dick Nixon being President of the United States," said Rockefeller as his vast teams pondered the landscape from the governor's offices on West Fifty-fifth Street in Manhattan. Concerned and savvy, Nixon even sent a young aide named John Ehrlichman to follow Governor Rocky around to public events and report back on the New Yorker's appeal. Two years earlier, in 1958, the *Time* headline about Rockefeller had read "Rocky on a Roll." Nixon's great fear was that that roll might take the governor from New York to the presidency of the nation.

Governor Rockefeller's planned roll westward was only one of two overriding Nixon obsessions heading into 1960. When Nixon's mind's eye shifted from New York to Arizona, from the seaboard to the Sunbelt, he had to reckon with the right's exploding star, Barry Goldwater. Handsome and bold, Goldwater took over his father's profitable department store business in Phoenix. A pilot, Goldwater flew missions in World War II and embraced a kind of Western self-reliant conservatism that was the antithesis of Roosevelt's New Deal. He was elected to the city council in Phoenix after the war and rose to the U.S. Senate. As a merchant in the 1930s, infuriated by an increase in the minimum wage and a limitation on working hours, Goldwater had written an open letter to President Roosevelt that brimmed with self-confident anger: "My friend, you have, for over five years, been telling me about your plans; how much they were going to do and how much they were going to mean to me," Goldwater wrote. "Now I want to turn around and ask you just what they have done that would be of any value to me as a businessman and a citizen. . . . I would like to know just where you are leading us. I like the old-fashioned way of being an American a lot better than the way we are headed for now."

Roosevelt would not be the last sitting president Goldwater would attack. In April 1957 the senator was asked to lunch at the White House to discuss his approaching reelection campaign. Goldwater did what almost no one ever does: he turned down a White House invitation. "No, he did not think it would be right for him to come to lunch," *Time* reported. "Why? On that very afternoon he planned to make a speech on the Senate floor bitterly attacking the White House concept of 'Modern Republicanism' and President Eisenhower's $71.8 billion budget."

It was a tough speech. The administration, Goldwater said, had been seduced by the "siren song of socialism" and was veering toward "squanderbust government . . . economic inebriation . . . [and] bloated government." Eisenhowerism, Goldwater declared, meant that Americans should be "federally born, federally housed, federally clothed, federally educated, federally supported in their occupations, and die a federal death, thereafter to be buried in a federal box in a federal cemetery."

Now, on the eve of the Republican convention in Chicago in 1960, Goldwater was even more firmly at the center of the conservatives' universe. As copies of *The Conscience of a Conservative* spread across college campuses and inside Rotary Clubs, the man with his name on the cover became for the right what Rockefeller was to the left: the conquering hero.

Nixon spent the first half of 1960 obsessively scheming to keep the nomination prize out of other men's hands. Trying to chart a course between Rockefeller and Goldwater, the vice president, with his raw, intuitive feel for politics, understood that a national victory would require an approach that was more centrist than overtly conservative. Nixon's instinctive right-wing streak—the streak that had brought him to national fame and to the national ticket in 1952— was only one of many streaks running through his complex personal and political makeup. Few American politicians have been so ambitious, so varied, so capable of stops and starts on issues foreign and domestic, than Richard Nixon. "There is something perhaps especially Californian about this strange Nixon uncertainty—and the manner in which the apparently firm and resolute man suddenly changes course and takes new directions," observed Teddy White. "It is as if the changing unsettled society of Southern California in which he grew up had imparted to him some of its own essential uncertainty." Teddy White did not note the darker truth that at the center of Nixon's tumultuous and chaotic political makeup was a manic drive for power and acceptance. For Nixon, charting a course between two political neophytes came instinctively to him.

What White saw as uncertainty and what others saw as ruthlessness, played itself out practically as an essential pragmatism, a way of looking at the world not as how it should be, but instead how it actually was. Nixon had been obsessively planning his presidential campaign for a long time—certainly longer than Rockefeller had after deciding almost flippantly to give politics a "whirl." Soon enough, the far-reaching efficacy of that planning was revealed.

The Rockefeller forces were surprised to find that not only were the best political operatives around the country largely unavailable to them, but so, too, were many business leaders. "These people liked

Ike," a Rockefeller intimate told Teddy White. "But they liked Nixon even more. Here was a boy who would continue the Eisenhower policies, who was not only very able but also amenable. They thought Nelson was too brilliant and unpredictable; Nelson's money hurt him because he didn't need them—he was too independent."

After an embarrassing national tour where he had sought support for an upcoming presidential bid, Nelson Rockefeller limped home in the last days of the 1950s and announced that he would *not* run for the GOP nomination, stepping out of the drama. Of course, the New York governor's arrogance and unpredictability would not allow him to stay on the sidelines for long. By the late spring of 1960 there was talk of a draft-Rockefeller movement. Rising tensions with the Soviets after a U.S. spy plane was shot down over Soviet airspace, and a summit collapsed, changed the national mood, raising anxieties about the direction of the country. By early summer, in the weeks running up to the Republican National Convention, Rockefeller issued a nine-point attack on the Eisenhower administration, framing his critique in terms virtually identical to John Kennedy's language on the Democratic side. "A new period now begins, and it summons new men," said Rockefeller. "New problems demand new ideas, new action. . . . I cannot pretend to believe that the Republican Party has fully met its duty."

In the weeks leading up to the Republican convention, Vice President Nixon remained pinned in from left and right. In hearings to hammer out the party's platform at the Blackstone Hotel in Chicago, Charles Percy of Illinois was left with the unenviable task of trying to keep proceedings moving even as party loyalties were split in three separate directions between Goldwater on the right, Rockefeller on the left, and Nixon in the center. The Illinois senator gamely tried, but it was a great challenge as hearts and minds were torn between wings of the party. "If we weren't concerned with winning, our sympathies would be almost unanimously with Goldwater," a "high convention official" said.

Rockefeller carried with him a hardwired sense of entitlement that made it impossible for the New York governor to slip quietly offstage at the Chicago convention. Nixon understood that and began working tirelessly to bring Rocky into the fold. For Nixon, victory would require both wings, but as a matter of crude political calculus he believed conservatives had no other choice but to side with him in November. In what later generations of American pols would call a "change" election, Nixon could defeat Jack Kennedy only if he reached more moderates and independents in the general election. With his more progressive views, Rockefeller's positions were more aligned with those swing voters. And so the conservatives, Nixon decided, would have to come along for the ride with Rockefeller whether they liked it or not.

Any hopes of a conservative on the ticket were dashed with Kennedy's choice of Lyndon Johnson for vice president. Nixon's hopes of leveraging conservative support in the Old Confederacy to crack the Democrats' Solid South—the Democrats were then the party of segregation—was made nearly impossible with the addition of a Texan who had chastised Nixon in 1957 for taking too expansive a view of civil rights. With a powerful Sun Belt senator on the Democratic ticket, the Solid South seemed to be safely in Democratic hands for another four years.

Now confronted with an electoral map that seemed to put New England and the South in the Democratic column, Nixon had to find a way to carry New York (forty-five electoral votes) and more moderate voters in large Northeast industrial states. The key to that support, Nixon believed, was not with a firebrand Arizona senator but instead with a governor of New York firmly ensconced in the Northeast establishment.

With all this in mind, the vice president of the United States secretly boarded a plane in Washington to fly to New York City on Friday, July 22, 1960. He'd called Herbert Brownell, the old Dewey hand and former Eisenhower attorney general, to see if he could set up a conversation with Rockefeller. "Tell Dick to call me," Rocky said to Brownell. Rocky would love to see Nixon, but only on home turf. As Friday afternoon waned, then, Nixon was heading for the governor of New York's massive Fifth Avenue apartment, whose walls were lined with priceless modern art. Nixon would dine with Governor Rockefeller in a last-ditch effort to get the liberal Republican onboard.

One of their first matters of business was whether Rockefeller would consent to run with Nixon in November. Earlier, Nixon had asked Eisenhower for help in persuading Rockefeller to become the vice presidential running mate. But Ike declined. "I don't see very well how I can get down on my knees to him," he said. "He is apparently possessed of a popular appeal that people feel—but he is no philosophical genius. He has a personal ambition that is overwhelming."

Now, high atop Manhattan's Upper East Side, pressing his point passionately, Nixon failed to move Rockefeller on the question. "I restated my position that I was not available in any circumstances," said Rockefeller, "and he restated his position that he would respect my feelings on the matter." (Stymied, in the end Nixon stayed in the

Rockefeller wing and region by choosing for his vice presidential running mate Henry Cabot Lodge of Massachusetts. Lodge, reported his Harvard roommate, had "commenced as a conservative and thawed into a progressive.")

The conversation then turned to the platform. Hours passed and Rockefeller bombarded Nixon with a flurry of demands regarding the party document. By midnight the two were ready to dictate changes to the work of the platform committee back in Chicago. A conference call was set up between Nixon, who sat at Rockefeller's desk; the governor himself; Charles Percy, in Chicago; and a Rockefeller aide who was also in Chicago. When all of Rockefeller's demands were met and all the platform changes were confirmed, at twenty minutes after three in the morning, Nixon boarded a chartered jet and flew back to Washington.

Rockefeller, meanwhile, could hardly contain himself and early the next morning issued a press release.

The Vice-President and I met today at my home in New York City. The meeting took place at the Vice-President's request. The purpose of the meeting was to discuss the platform of the Republican Party.

On fourteen succeeding points, Rockefeller announced, the two men had come to agreement, and the result was a critique of Eisenhower on defense and the assertion of more progressive principles on civil rights and health care, arguing for "aggressive action to remove the remaining vestiges of segregation or discrimination in all areas of national life—voting and housing, schools and jobs" and coverage of "health insurance for the aged."

Rocky was exactly where he wanted to be, at center stage shouting out instructions. "If you don't think that represents my views," the governor said, "you're crazy." It was a good thing for Nixon that at least the New York governor was pleased by his work, because few others were. Ike was deeply insulted by the attacks on his foreign policy. The chairman of the Texas delegation, Thad Hutcheson, called the "Compact of Fifth Avenue" a "damned sellout," which was mild compared to Barry Goldwater's reaction.

"I think the Republican Party would both be breaking faith with itself and shirking its duty to the nation should we fail to identify ourselves with the conservative point of view in both domestic and foreign affairs," said Goldwater. "Early today came the disturbing news that Mr. Nixon himself has felt it necessary to make overtures and concessions to the liberals. . . . I believe this to be immoral politics. I also believe it to be self-defeating. . . . Alienate the conservatives—as the party is now in the process of doing—and the handful of liberal militants that are seeking to take over the Republican Party will inherit a mess of pottage." Should the agreement between Rockefeller and Nixon be allowed to stand, Goldwater said, "it will live in history as the Munich of the Republican Party. It will be a Munich in two senses, that it subordinated principle to expediency; and that it guaranteed precisely the evil it was designed to prevent—in this case a Republican defeat in November."

After the Compact of Fifth Avenue, Nixon spent the next few weeks in cleanup mode as Goldwater was thundering at him from the right and Eisenhower was attacking from the center. The sitting president, and Nixon's boss, called his vice president from Newport to express disapproval over the defense elements of the deal with Rockefeller. Nixon tried to placate the old man, saying, "What I'm trying to do is find some ground on which this fellow [Rockefeller] can be with us and not against us," he told the president.

Nixon struggled to find that middle way, directing the platform to finally read: "The United States can and must provide whatever is necessary to insure its own security . . . to provide any necessary increased expenditures to meet new situations. . . . To provide more would be wasteful. To provide less would be catastrophic."

Time approved of Nixon's kowtowing on Fifth Avenue, calling the veep's trip to Rockefeller's apartment a "bold stroke" and praising it as a breakthrough moment in the campaign.

With brilliant timing and tactics, Richard Nixon had used the meeting with Rockefeller to position himself on the side of new departures for the 1960s, broadening his potential appeal to independent voters, without losing the value of identification with the Eisenhower Administration record—a record that got a considerable boost last week from the announcement of a billion-dollar budget surplus and the successful shot of the new Polaris missile from a submerged submarine. Yet by easing the GOP platform in the directions that Nelson Rockefeller had urged, Nixon largely cancelled out the political appeal of the Democratic platform, and made the GOP platform what he wanted to make it—an elective basis for his campaign and a point of departure for the challenging decade ahead.

Nixon himself could not have written a more favorable summary. Conservatives were enraged but were operating from a less advantageous position than Rockefeller Republicans. There had been a late effort to draft Goldwater at the convention but the Arizona senator's forces were unable to nail down a single significant supporter. They instead were left grousing for years to come about how Richard Nixon's shameless lurch left may have ensured him the nomination but ended up costing him the White House.

Had Nixon run as a full-throated conservative, the argument goes, perhaps the outcome would have been different. In the end, though, even Goldwater saw—or said he saw—the wisdom of Nixon's approach. In his own formal speech to the Republican convention in Chicago, Goldwater put away his talk of Munich and spoke in more practical terms. "Now, radical Democrats, who rightfully fear that the American people will reject their extreme program in November, are watching this convention with eager hope that some split may occur in our party," Goldwater told the delegates. "I am telling them now that no such split will take place. Let them know that the conservatives of the Republican Party do not intend by any act of theirs to turn this country over, by default, to a party which has lost its belief in the dignity of man, a party which has no faith in our economic system, a party which has come to the belief that the United States is a second-rate power."

The Arizonan spoke sharply to his ideological brethren within the party. "We don't gain anything when you get mad at a candidate because you don't agree with his every philosophy," Goldwater said. "We don't gain anything when you disagree with the platform and then do not go out and work and vote for your party. I know what you say, 'I will get even with that fellow. I will show this party something.' But what are you doing when you stay at home? You are help-ing the opposition party elect candidates dedicated to the destruction of this country."

For all the sound and fury from the right and left in the days lead-ing up to the 1960 Republican convention, it is worth noting that the party gave Richard Nixon the 1960 presidential nomination in over-whelming fashion. Eisenhower's vice president received all conven-tion votes except for the ten cast by the delegation from Louisiana, who went on record in favor of Barry Goldwater for president. Just as scientists and philosophers speculate on how the flight of a single butterfly can cause a hurricane, political observers have speculated on that symbolic gesture of calling for a Goldwater presidential campaign on a July night in Chicago in 1960, and how it would in the coming months and years prefigure one of the most formidable storms in political history, the 1964 contest for the Republican nom-ination.

After John Kennedy's inaugural ceremonies, Nixon and his wife, Pat, attended a farewell luncheon for the Eisenhowers at the F Street Club. The Nixons dined at home that evening with family. After-ward the now former vice president asked his driver, John Wardlaw, to take him on a final drive. "The streets were snarled with traffic, made worse by the snow and ice," Nixon recalled in his memoirs. "Hundreds of cars and rented limousines were lined up outside the hotels, waiting to pick up men in tails and women in long gowns on their way to the inaugural balls." Nixon could not keep his melan-choly at bay. "No one noticed us as we drove past the White House and headed through the streets to Capitol Hill."

Once at the Capitol, the lonely Nixon took a stroll through the building's empty halls, through the Rotunda, and out to a balcony that looked west across the capital. It was, Nixon recalled, beautiful. There was snow, and the monuments to Washington and to Lincoln stood majestically in the night.

He, too, stood for a time—perhaps five minutes, gazing out at the prize that had only just eluded his grasp. He looked neither left nor right, but straight ahead, down the center of the Mall.

He knew he would be back.

"I walked as fast as I could back to the car," Nixon wrote. There was no time to waste.

3

Goldwater, Extremism, and the Rise of LBJ

"In your heart you know he's right."
—*Pro-Goldwater slogan, 1964*

"In your guts you know he's nuts."
—*Anti-Goldwater slogan, 1964*

IN HIS SEQUEL TO THE PULITZER PRIZE—WINNING *MAKING of the President 1960*, Teddy White put the problem of 1964 well. "The election of 1960 could have been called by no man a Republican disaster," White wrote. "The tiny, almost invisible margin of Democratic victory made it the closest run in American history. But the very narrowness of the defeat had brought on Richard M. Nixon the most violent abuse of both wings of his Party—if he had just made this speech, they chanted, or taken this position, they complained, or adjusted his stance that mite, said both his enemies and former friends, victory might have been his."

It was a lingering angst that both Al Gore and John Kerry would endure for years following their painful losses to George W. Bush in 2000 and 2004. Gore's suffering, like Nixon's in 1960, would be amplified by his own party's endless speculation over why he distanced himself from Bill Clinton, or moderated on gun control and environmental issues, or fumbled his three debates with Bush, or gave up the fight for Florida too early, or . . .

Every politician who puts his or her name on a ballot signs up to endure a lifetime of second-guessing. As the White House tapes so depressingly illustrate, Nixon never passed up a single resentment or grudge in his political life. The unending chatter about how he could have and should have won against JFK would drive him to distraction for the rest of his life. His rivalry with his fellow Navy vet would endure even to the final, darkest day of Nixon's political life. As he struggled to put together the words of his final address as president of the American people, Nixon's mind locked onto his resentment for the now martyred Kennedy. Even Kennedy's mother, Rose, had warranted a biography. "Nobody will ever write a book, probably, about my mother." Nixon said. "Well, I guess all of you would say this about your mother—my mother was a saint." A saint, perhaps, but little consolation to a man who collected resentments like FDR collected stamps. And that collection of resentments seemed forever fixed on that shattering loss in 1960.

I sympathize with Nixon's anguish over that razor-thin defeat. There are many explanations for why Nixon lost and Kennedy won—and a number of those reasons begin and end in Cook County, Illinois, and their sketchy vote-counting schemes. But in the annals of modern conservatism the principal cause for this Republican loss is said to be that Nixon doomed himself by turned himself into a Rockefeller Republican. I don't think so. That argument proves flimsy when held up to the light of election results in the eight years preceding 1960 and the presidential elections eight years after. For

what worked for Nixon in 1968 and 1972 had also worked spectacularly for Ike in 1952 and 1956. The same approach came up short by
the narrowest of margins in 1960, but Goldwater worshippers saw
an opening and were determined to exploit it, and prove to GOP
leaders that the outcome would be radically different four years later
with a hardline conservative at the top of the ticket. They didn't
know how right they were, as radically different it would be.

Nineteen sixty-four gave conservatives a chance to show skeptics
what they were made of. And while the long-term impact of Goldwater's 1964 crusade would in many ways transform the Republican
Party, the practical impact on presidential politics as measured by
votes gained in a national election was exceedingly grim.

But so, too, was the mood in the United States leading up to Goldwater's run for president. From Dallas to Vietnam to Birmingham,
there was too much bloodshed in 1963 and 1964. To understand
Goldwater's quixotic run for the White House, and the inspiring
movement it launched, we have to first understand the cultural
earthquake that was under way all across America on the eve of the
'64 election.

Events across America were far more tumultuous than usual in
1963. The civil rights movement gave America a running passion
play in the bloodstained streets of the South, where Southern blacks
nonviolently submitted to brutality at the hands of angry white po-
licemen, snarling dogs, and fire hoses. In September a bomb tore
through the Sixteenth Street Baptist Church in Birmingham, killing
four little girls. It was a savage attack that would connect the cause
of civil rights with the mainstream of American voters.

Meanwhile, the fears of a Cold War turning nuclear hung heavy in hearts across the country. Right-wing demonstrators in Texas had to be restrained from attacking U.N. ambassador Adlai Stevenson; even Lady Bird Johnson was jostled by an angry crowd. Newspaper ads greeted JFK's 1963 trip to Dallas by suggesting his administration was sympathetic to Moscow while handbills circulated throughout the city accusing the president of treason against the United States of America.

And then the shots rang out in Dealey Plaza on that spectacularly sunny Texas afternoon, murdering the young president of the United States in plain daylight.

A half century later, the effect of the assassination of John Fitzgerald Kennedy on *everything* that has come since is difficult to overstate. The question of what might have happened had President Kennedy lived will be debated as long as there is an America. Would we have fought the way we did in Vietnam? Would the federal government have come under such sustained and successful attack if the Democrat managing the 1960s had been the more cautious John Kennedy rather than the more ambitious Lyndon Johnson? Would the cause of civil rights have proceeded on a more gradual pace under JFK?

We'll never know. What's clear is that the assassination and Johnson's legislative reaction to it did two things that shaped the campaign of 1964 and all subsequent American history. In the wake of Dallas, the new president moved immediately—beginning with his very first speech to the Congress after Kennedy's funeral—to take up the cause of the civil rights bill that Kennedy had proposed but which had been stalled before the murder.

Pressing for the historic legislation, Johnson was self-consciously attempting to take his place in the pantheon of presidential greats. Here was a Texan, a white Southerner who was a former opponent of civil rights legislation, fulfilling the legacy of his slain predecessor by finishing the work first undertaken by the first and greatest Republican president, Abraham Lincoln.

In a season of vote getting, cajoling, and deal making that stretched even Lyndon Johnson's Olympian skills of manipulation to new lengths, the president heard history's trumpets even amid the tactical chaos of the first half of 1964. In the end, as June turned into July, Johnson is said to have remarked to an aide that by signing the civil rights bill he had just turned the South over to the Republican Party for a generation. He was wrong, as it turned out: GOP dominance over the Old Confederacy was to last for two generations with the notable exceptions of Jimmy Carter's and Bill Clinton's three successful presidential campaigns. But it wasn't until Barack Obama carried Virginia, North Carolina, and Florida in 2008 that the Solid South began to transition into a region once again in play. In fact, it speaks to the GOP's current ills that Florida, Virginia, North Carolina, Georgia, Louisiana, Arkansas, and Kentucky remain in play in presidential politics to this day.

Lyndon Johnson signed the 1964 Civil Rights Act on July 2. It was a watershed moment, one that had been foreshadowed in 1948 when young Hubert Humphrey told the Democratic National Convention in Philadelphia that one day Americans would walk in the "sunshine" of racial equality—a speech that sent Strom Thurmond out the door of the Democratic Party, leading to the Dixiecrat revolt that would in turn lead to the end of Democrats' dominance in the Deep South.

One Republican vote against the bill in the Senate was to loom large in the coming months: that of Barry Goldwater, the gentleman from Arizona.

Goldwater's vote on civil rights carried a historic significance for Republican candidates not just in 1964 but also for the five decades that followed. Just four years before that civil rights vote, Richard Nixon had carried 32 percent of the African American vote, traditionally a GOP stronghold since Abraham Lincoln freed the slaves a century earlier. But after Goldwater became the party's nominee, his opposition to LBJ's civil rights legislation helped contribute to a massive falloff of support from African Americans. Goldwater carried 6 percent of the black vote that year and in the fifty years that have followed, Republican nominees for president have rarely seen their support from African Americans rise above 10 percent.

The presumptive nominee of the Republican Party had gone on record opposing integrated public accommodations, and blacks around the nation were confronted with a striking reversal of political reality. For generations, large numbers of African Americans had seen the Republicans as their defenders. In the century following the Civil War's end in 1865, it was Democratic Party leaders across the South that fiercely protected segregation, creating a white Solid South dominated by the party of FDR. Blacks hoping for an end to segregation saw no need to vote Democratic.

But in the presidential race of 1964, Democrats moved from oppressor to deliverer. Republicans, whose view of civil rights was bound up with their ever-deepening skepticism of the federal government, were moving into active resistance to the kinds of racial, social, and cultural changes promised on a national level by those politicians supporting integration. To most voters in 1964, that position was nothing less than the fulfillment of the premise, immortalized in the Declaration of Independence, that all men were created equal. To Barry Goldwater and many movement conservatives, on the other hand, the civil rights bills did great violence to the Tenth Amendment and its reservation of rights to the states, federalism, and the right of individuals to run their communities as they wished. Always potent, the politics of race took on a new form as Republicans in the summer of 1964 began to turn their attention toward attracting white Democrats who might be disaffected by Johnson's reordering of the national agenda.

The rise of "movement conservatives" was built on a simple creed of anticommunism and individual rights. William F. Buckley had stated his case and that of the modern political movement he helped create when he wrote in 1959:

> I will not cede more power to the state. I will not willingly cede more power to anyone, not to the state, not to General Motors, not to the CIO. I will hoard my power like a miser, resisting every effort to drain it away from me. I will then use my power, as I see fit. I mean to live my life an obedient man, but obedient to God, subservient to the wisdom of my ancestors; never to the authority of political truths arrived at yesterday at the voting booth. That is a program of sorts, is it not? It is certainly program enough to keep conservatives busy, and liberals at bay. And the nation free.

That freedom from federal entanglements meant to Buckley and a generation of conservatives in 1964 the freedom to sell your home to whomever you wished, the freedom to run your local schools as you wished, and the right to choose which customers you wanted to serve and which you did not.

Buckley and his *National Review* would oppose the Civil Rights Acts of 1964 and 1965 as a reaction against the expansion of Washington power, but soon after Goldwater's defeat Buckley changed course saying it was a mistake for *National Review* to oppose civil rights legislation. Like many others on both sides of the political divide, he was deeply offended by the violence unleashed against civil rights activists and was openly contemptuous of George Wallace's run for the White House in 1968 and 1972. By the mid-1960s, Bill Buckley served notice that segregationists were no more welcome in his conservative movement than members of the John Birch Society or disciples of Ayn Rand.

In the lead-up to the 1964 debacle, Barry Goldwater remained a reluctant warrior who persistently resisted, privately and genuinely, a presidential campaign. But even the impassioned senator could not deny a conservative crusade that was quickly becoming inevitable. In 1962 he published a follow-up to *The Conscience of a Conservative* entitled *Why Not Victory? A Fresh Look at American Foreign Policy.* The "fresh look" was unsurprisingly and unapologetically hawkish. The Eisenhower policy of controlling military spending and minimizing the use of bellicose rhetoric toward the Soviets gave Goldwater a huge pivot point to argue that the U.S. policy of "containment" was too weak an approach. Confrontation, not coexistence, was at the heart of Goldwater's vision and it was a position that would later be adopted by the Republican president whose willingness to confront the Soviet Union in the 1980s helped bring an end to the Cold War.

Across America, young volunteers seemed ready to answer the call of the conservative movement's conscience. A movement in support of Goldwater's nomination in 1964 had begun through what later generations would call "micro-targeting." Those efforts had been quietly (and sometimes not so quietly) under way since 1961. F. Clifton White may not be a household name, even in the households of political junkies, but he should be. Working with other conservatives, White was struggling to master the delegate math in order to make a Goldwater nomination possible. White slowly and carefully expanded the circle of his conspirators, once convening the group at a hunting lodge in Minnesota. His reasons for the retreat were practical: "I wanted them to spend two days together and not only talk, but drink whiskey together, and get to know each other, and be friends and trust each other," White said.

In early 1964, when the campaign for the Republican nomination began in earnest, primaries had not yet come into their current prominence; a few contests were used as pre-convention proxies. In New Hampshire, a quasi–favorite son, Henry Cabot Lodge, won the race to little fanfare or consequence. After a hard-fought campaign in Oregon, Nelson Rockefeller launched his campaign in defense of what he called "the mainstream" of Republican voters. (Rocky had been hurt by his divorce and remarriage; the mores that would allow Ronald Reagan to become the first divorced man to be elected president or Newt Gingrich to win the 2012 South Carolina primary had not yet shifted.) At least in the Pacific Northwest, that moderate message carried the day. In California, though, Goldwater pulled off a victory, proving he could win elections in large states outside of

Arizona. But even a primary victory in a state as significant as California carried little significance in the drive for the party's nomination. That would be decided at the national convention by a collection of party leaders and delegates who had long cast a wary eye toward Barry Goldwater and his rabid band of followers.

It's the rare national party convention that endures in memory. For those of us who love politics, there are, happily, exceptions. For Democrats the chaos of Chicago in 1968 and Miami in 1972 stand out. For Republicans, Ronald Reagan's challenge to a sitting president in 1976 and, of course, Barry Goldwater's ascent in the GOP's 1964 San Francisco convention. That gathering in the City by the Bay vividly displayed what had been real but less evident so far in the post–World War II period: the GOP was fractured and its leading interests were either unwilling or unable to bring about the kind of political unity that is required to win a general election.

The convention, held at the Cow Palace in San Francisco, was raw. The delegates roared in fury at Nelson Rockefeller, who felt the need to remind the raucous party of Lincoln "it's still a free country."

One sign of just how on edge voters were in San Francisco—and across the country in this time of riots and rumors of riots—was President Eisenhower's speech to the delegates. The former "moderate" president warned against "maudlin sympathy for the criminal who, roaming the streets with a switchblade knife and illegal firearms seeking a helpless prey, suddenly becomes upon apprehension a poor, underprivileged person who counts upon the compassion of our society and the laxness or weaknesses of too many courts to forgive his offense."

While Ike's tough words still help explain a country on edge a half century later, the convention will be forever remembered for Barry Goldwater's barnstorming acceptance speech.

"The Good Lord raised this mighty Republic . . . not to stagnate in the swamplands of collectivism, not to cringe before the bully of Communism," said Goldwater.

Goldwater was building up to the political punch line that would hammer the consciousness of the country.

"Extremism in the defense of liberty is no vice," said Goldwater, and *"moderation in the pursuit of justice is no virtue."*

"Extremism" had a particular meaning at that moment. At the convention Rockefeller had been pushing for a plank denouncing the John Birchers and other marginally ideological groups that even Buckley had attacked, and the battle internally had come to be known as the "extremism" issue. Rather than keeping a healthy political distance from such forces—the chief wish of the moderate and liberal wings of the party—Goldwater chose instead to use his acceptance speech to make it plain that he was going to dance with the ones that had brought him to the nomination: the hard-core conservatives. In a famous anecdote, a reporter turned to Teddy White after hearing the line in the Cow Palace and remarked, "My God, he's going to run as Barry Goldwater."

On the day after the speech, Goldwater held fast to his uncompromising approach. Responding to criticism from Rockefeller over the "extremism" language, Goldwater said, "I would like the Governor, for my benefit and the benefit of the party and of the people of America, to put down in writing his definition of extremism. Extremism is no sin if you are engaged in the defense of freedom." It was a clarion call for conservatives who would be drubbed in 1964 but rise again to victory nationwide in the 1966 midterm elections.

During the San Francisco convention, Goldwater paid a courtesy call on President Eisenhower at the St. Francis Hotel to gain the blessing of the man he had verbally abused on the campaign trail in years past. Given Ike's pride and Goldwater's independence, it is not surprising that the session produced no apparent impetus toward unifying the traditional party base that had been a hallmark of Eisenhower's success in the 1952 and 1956 elections. To John S. Knight, the head of the Knight newspaper chain, Goldwater remarked that he had "no immediate plans" to pull the GOP's wings together to push for victory in November. Yes, he believed the party could unite, but the task was apparently far from a priority for the nominee. This was less a campaign than it was an ideological crusade.

The autumn campaign was predictably harsh. In early September the Johnson campaign aired the "Daisy" ad, in which a two-year-old girl's counting of daisy petals morphs into a nuclear countdown and then a mushroom cloud before Johnson's voice says: "These are the stakes! To make a world in which all of God's children can live, or to go into the dark. We must either love each other, or we must die."

Johnson's crude approach offended viewers and the ad was taken off the air, but Goldwater was making Johnson's path to victory much easier than it should have been. The Republican nominee had mused about making Social Security voluntary, talked about the tactical use of nuclear weapons in Southeast Asia, wondered aloud about giving field commanders the power to use nukes, advocated the selling of the Tennessee Valley Authority (while in Tennessee!).

The Goldwater campaign was a grand adventure for the candidate and his true believers, a chance to barnstorm the country making the conservative case on matters foreign and domestic. It was the movement's chance, at last, to show those staid, starched men who ran the Grand Old Party how to run an insurgent campaign for president without making Nixonian compromises with moderates.

This great adventure may have been an exhilarating political experiment for the conservative base, but the 1964 campaign was not a plausible effort to win an electoral majority or a mandate to govern. In endorsing President Johnson for reelection, *The Atlantic Monthly*, then published in Boston, gave clear voice to the view of the establishment. "In his drive for the nomination, and ever since, Senator Goldwater has accepted the proposition that a ruthless minority taking over first the Republican Party and then the nation shall break with the past as it chooses," the magazine said. *The Atlantic* decried Goldwater's "proposal to let field commanders have their choice of the smaller nuclear weapons," arguing that such a policy "would rupture a fundamental belief that has existed from Abraham Lincoln to today: the belief that in times of crisis the civilian authority must have control over the military." The GOP nominee's "preference to let states like Mississippi, Alabama, and Georgia enforce civil rights within their own borders" was popular, *The Atlantic* noted, with George Wallace, the Ku Klux Klan, and the John Birchers. Finally, on the diplomatic plane, the Goldwater "threat to walk out of the United Nations if he does not approve of its action is a repudiation of what the best brains, Republican and Democrat, have helped to contribute to that peace-keeping institution." By the end of October, far more Americans sided with *The Atlantic Monthly*'s view of the election than the *National Review*'s.

Sixty-one percent of the Americans who voted on Election Day 1964 chose Lyndon Johnson in the second greatest landslide in U.S. history. Only Franklin Roosevelt enjoyed a greater percentage of the popular vote than Johnson did on that day. The man and his movement who had been so openly contemptuous of Richard Nixon after he lost to JFK by a tally of 49.72 percent to 49.55 percent got obliterated in every region of the country and lost to Johnson by over 20 percentage points.

The conventional wisdom after the failed 1964 experiment was virtually unanimous—and almost unanimously wrong.

"Barry Goldwater not only lost the presidential election yesterday," wrote James Reston in *The New York Times*, "but the conservative cause as well. He has wrecked his party for a long time to come."

But even Johnson's thunderous win failed to quiet a roiling nation. Writing in the October 1964 issue of *Harper's*, Richard Hofstadter, the Columbia University political scientist, described what he called "The Paranoid Style in American Politics," a feature of the extremes of both right and left.

"The paranoid spokesman sees the fate of conspiracy in apocalyptic terms—he traffics in the birth and death of whole worlds, whole political orders, whole systems of human values," wrote Hofstadter. "He is always manning the barricades of civilization. He constantly lives at a turning point. Like religious millennialists he expresses the anxiety of those who are living through the last days and he is sometimes disposed to set a date for the apocalypse. ('Time is running out,' said [John Birch Society founder Robert] Welch in 1951. 'Evidence is piling up on many sides and from many sources that October 1952 is the fatal month when Stalin will attack.')"

In the conclusion to the article that was written a half century ago but could explain the mind-set of too many cable news and talk radio hosts, Internet bloggers, and a certain Nobel Prize–winning economist today, Hofstadter wrote:

Perhaps the central situation conducive to the diffusion of the paranoid tendency is a confrontation of opposed interests which are (or are felt to be) totally irreconcilable, and thus by nature not susceptible to the normal political processes of bargain and compromise. The situation becomes worse when the representatives of a particular social interest—perhaps because of the very unrealistic and unrealizable nature of its demands—are shut out of the political process. Having no access to political bargaining or the making of decisions, they find their original conception that the world of power is sinister and malicious fully confirmed. They see only the consequences of power—and this through distorting lenses—and have no chance to observe its actual machinery. A distinguished historian has said that one of the most valuable things about history is that it teaches us how things do not happen. It is precisely this kind of awareness that the paranoid fails to develop. He has a special resistance of his own, of course, to developing such awareness, but circumstances often deprive him of exposure to events that might enlighten him—and in any case he resists enlightenment. We are all sufferers from history, but the paranoid is a double sufferer, since

*he is afflicted not only by the real world, with the rest of us, but
by his fantasies as well.*

The same month Hofstadter's wise piece on the psychological
roots and practical perils of extremism appeared, Goldwater's campaign underwrote a broadcast in the waning days of the election that
featured a man of whom many things could be—and had been, and
surely were to be—said. But no one in their right mind could call
him paranoid.

Ronald Wilson Reagan was a true believing conservative, but he
was hardly an extremist—and though liberals could not yet be sure
of it, that combination of conviction and polish were about to launch
one of the greatest political stories in American history. It's a story,
in fact, that is still unfurling.

4

Reagan's Rendezvous with Destiny

"You know I'm running against an actor. Remember this, you know who shot Abraham Lincoln, don't you?"
—*Edmund G. "Pat" Brown*

"Today, more than ever, it is necessary to proceed with change with the greatest care."
—*Ronald Reagan*

It began simply.

"Thank you," Reagan said.

Thank you very much. Thank you and good evening. The sponsor has been identified, but unlike most television programs, the performer hasn't been provided with a script. As a matter of fact, I have been permitted to choose my own words and discuss my own ideas regarding the choice that we face in the next few weeks.

Reagan let his audience know right up front that "nobody's written my script and tonight nobody is paying me to talk." He began with a flair of independence straight out of the West.

I have spent most of my life as a Democrat. I recently have seen fit to follow another course. I believe that the issues confronting us cross party lines.

Here Reagan is telling many of his listeners—the ever-growing "Silent Majority"—that he's one of them. He knows what it's like to have worshipped FDR but now feel the Democratic Party has become overrun with people who mock their values and despise their middle-class worldview.

As for the peace that we would preserve, I wonder who among us would like to approach the wife or mother whose husband or son has died in South Vietnam and ask them if they think this is a peace that should be maintained indefinitely. Do they mean peace, or do they mean we just want to be left in peace? There can be no real peace while one American is dying some place in the world for the rest of us.

Reagan's call for strength and courage in America's fight against Communism would ground his foreign policy for the next quarter century but on this night, the actor was telling Americans that they could not escape history. We're at war in Vietnam, he was reminding them. Why pretend we're not?

This is the issue of this election: Whether we believe in our capacity for self-government or whether we abandon the American revolution and confess that a little intellectual elite in a far-distant capital can plan our lives for us better than we can plan them ourselves.

This is the essence of the modern conservative doctrine: shouldn't we run our own lives instead of Washington elites?

No government ever voluntarily reduces itself in size. So governments' programs, once launched, never disappear. Actually, a government bureau is the nearest thing to eternal life we'll ever see on this earth.

Another article of faith for the right: here Reagan uses wit to make a point that could seem harsh coming from someone else like Barry Goldwater—a great Reagan gift.

You and I have a rendezvous with destiny. We'll preserve for our children this, the last best hope of man on earth, or we'll sentence them to take the last step into a thousand years of darkness. We will keep in mind and remember that Barry Goldwater has faith in us. He has faith that you and I have the ability and the dignity and the right to make our own decisions and determine our own destiny. Thank you very much.

One thing was clear as Reagan closed his speech: it was Reagan himself who surely had a rendezvous with destiny.

A son of the Midwest, "Dutch" Reagan had lived a kind of golden life, remembering his Illinois childhood as idyllic despite his alcoholic father's occasional collapses on the front lawn. His mother, Nelle, was a force of nature, instilling in her sons (Reagan's older brother, Neil, was known as "Moon") a sense of religion and of drama.

His father's instability and the difficulty of making a living selling shoes led the Reagans to frequent moves, though Dutch was to spend much of his youth in Dixon, Illinois, where he played sports, acted in plays, and served as lifeguard on the Rock River, where he made seventy-seven notches on a log to mark the lives he saved.

At Eureka College from the fall of 1928 to the spring of 1932, Reagan cruised through some of the worst economic years in American history, earning money by washing dishes in his fraternity house, playing football, and dabbling in student politics, which he found fascinating. Reagan's natural skills as leader were so evident that when the students of Eureka launched a protest against the school, the seniors tapped a young seventeen-year-old freshman to lead the charge. When asked why seniors would pick a freshman like Reagan, Eureka senior Howard Short said, "There was just something special about the kid, a look in his eyes, he believed and he made you believe."

Almost four decades later, that seventeen-year-old kid would look into the eyes of the American people and make them believe that the genius of conservatism was more vital to the well-being of the Republic than ever before. Reagan's optimism in the face of the coming Goldwater disaster was infectious.

After graduating from Eureka in 1932, even the Great Depression couldn't keep Ronald Reagan down. He quickly found a radio job that combined two of his passions, sports and performing, and he became a skilled broadcaster. He did play-by-play for the Chicago Cubs. On a trip to Cubs spring training on Catalina Island in the glistening Pacific waters off Los Angeles, Reagan won a screen test with Warner Brothers and signed a movie contract. Only five years out of Eureka, then, and less than a decade away from living in Nelle and Jack Reagan's not-always-smooth household, Ronald Reagan landed a piece of the American Dream.

Much later, Reagan's political foes would accuse him of being a "chameleon," always taking on the characteristics of whatever company he was in. Part of this is just an actor's habit—great performers know their audiences—but there is no mistaking that Reagan joined the liberal Hollywood establishment lock, stock, and barrel in the late 1930s and 1940s. He described himself as a "hemophiliac liberal," bleeding sympathy for statist solutions to all of life's problems.

As the old joke goes, though, a conservative is a liberal who's been mugged by reality, and Reagan was mugged by both rising taxes and the fear of Communist influence in the movie business. He gradually moved right through the 1940s and 1950s and early 1960s but was reluctant to leave the party of FDR, his great hero. For years Reagan was the go-to guy if you wanted to form a "Democrats for Nixon" kind of committee.

When he finally changed his party affiliation, he completed a journey that was being replicated in households across America as working-class Democrats who never conceived that they might one day leave their party did just that.

Of course, as Reagan said innumerable times, he didn't leave the Democratic Party—the Democratic Party left him.

Understanding what he meant by this is key to understanding the enormous political shifts in the country in the 1960s and beyond. For so many of Reagan's generation, men and women who had come of age during the Great Depression and World War II, the party of Franklin Roosevelt was sacrosanct. It had been FDR's reassuring voice that had led them through the darkness of the 1930s and the cataclysm of the war; when he died at Warm Springs, Georgia, on April 12, 1945, millions of Americans commonly and genuinely likened it to a death in the family. For my mother's family in rural Georgia, the loss of Roosevelt was "like the passing of a beloved king."

"We thought the world would come to an end," I remember my mother telling me of her poor Southern family's response to the death of this man of great power and privilege.

Since George III Americans have always been skeptical of centralized authority and government control. FDR's genius lay in the way he managed to convince many of his countrymen—like my parents and grandparents—that during the most challenging of times, the public sector should be given the benefit of the doubt for the duration of those crises. His approach largely worked: though the Republicans of the time continued to champion Calvin Coolidge's belief in limited government, Republicans were irrelevant to national government throughout the 1930s and 1940s as Democrats won every presidential election between 1932 and 1948—a streak of five consecutive victories.

But as with Winston Churchill in Great Britain, victory in war brought change at home. Churchill was given thanks by the British people for saving Western Civilization from the scourge of Nazi tyranny by being unceremoniously run out of 10 Downing Street. Churchill's wife told her wounded hero that the loss was probably a blessing in disguise, to which the great man replied that the blessing seemed quite effectively disguised. But the postwar restlessness that was moving British politics toward a more centralized state was moving the United States in the opposite direction.

The conservative shift that began with Yalta was blending, in fact, into the American mainstream alongside a growing resistance to, and reaction against, the rise of domestic taxes and federal control that grew out of FDR's New Deal policies and extended beyond the end of the war. Truman's unpopularity led to the first GOP majority since Herbert Hoover was president and eight years of Ike ironically focused a new band of conservative "radicals" to tear away at New Deal policies. Social change throughout the 1950s and early 1960s was met with the same unease as the burgeoning civil rights movement. As riots swept through the country in 1964 and 1965, more Americans believed that the world they had created by winning the war twenty years earlier on the beaches of the Pacific and battlefields of Europe was now being destroyed by radical forces on college campuses and by riots in the heart of America's biggest cities.

Tensions between California law enforcement and the African American community in Watts exploded in the first days of August 1965, and before it was done five days later thirty-four people were dead, huge tracts of Los Angeles were in ashes, and all too many white Angelinos had gone out to buy guns in the event of a race war—a seemingly real prospect. Afterward the *Los Angeles Times* said that Watts was now "a holocaust of rubble and ruins not unlike the aftermath in London when the Nazis struck, or Berlin after Allied armies finished their demolition." To millions of Americans, the greatest outrage of this "holocaust" was that the damage was inflicted upon Los Angeles by radicalized black Americans within a week of Lyndon Johnson passing the landmark Voting Rights Act of 1965. LBJ had little time to savor the passing of that monumental piece of legislation. As helicopters beamed the images of Watts burning nationwide, Johnson's Great Society was finished and the rise of Reagan had begun.

As Reagan closed in on a gubernatorial run against incumbent Democratic governor Edmund G. "Pat" Brown in the 1966 campaign, the former actor spoke out against the radical social forces unleashed on California campuses and in support of law and order in the wake of Watts. Reagan, however, was extremely careful to avoid raw race-baiting. "White backlash" was the political phrase du jour in the mid-1960s, but Reagan, like the most successful Republican politicians, eschewed the type of racist appeals that propelled George Wallace and other Democrats to power in the Deep South.

Progressives writing the first several drafts of the 1960s political history have been so determined to explain away liberalism's humiliating collapse by pointing to a race-driven "Southern Strategy" that the cultural chaos facing middle-class voters during Reagan's sudden ascent is often overlooked. Beyond riots and civil rights legislation that sadly stirred racial resentments in some quarters of the electorate, radical societal shifts caused by a sexual revolution, violent antiwar protests, a growing drug culture, and open rebellion against the church, academia, and middle-class mores left millions of Americans believing that their country was falling apart. While the most violent action in this dizzying and discombobulating culture war unfolded in the streets of the cities, the crisis of order was surely not limited to Watts or Newark or Harlem. The culture wars that Pat Buchanan would refer to as late as 1992 were unfolding in white households across America, too, as this strange new cultural revolution spread from suburb to suburb.

While it is convenient for historians and liberal commentators to lay the collapse of Johnson liberalism at the feet of racist voters, this conveniently ignores the fact that LBJ won a historic landslide a year before Watts promising the type of civil rights legislation he passed a year later. It also whitewashes away the 70 percent approval rating the liberal president had as he was passing one piece of civil rights legislation after another in 1965. If race were at the heart of the Republican rise in the 1960s, LBJ's popularity would have plummeted long before the 1966 midterms. Ronald Reagan and Richard Nixon would also be no more appealing to such a large swath of voters than racist Democrats like George Wallace or Lester Maddox. The most laughable omission from liberal academics on this front may be that the man who is claimed to be the biggest beneficiary of a racist "Southern Strategy" was the same Republican presidential nominee to receive the highest percentage of the black vote in the last sixty years—Richard Nixon.

The appeal of Nixon and Reagan went well beyond the crudeness of segregationist populists who constituted the Democratic Party across the South for much of the twentieth century. LBJ himself fought against racial advancements for most of his congressional career and attacked Vice President Richard Nixon as late as 1957 for having an overly expansive view on the subject of civil rights legislation. Despite the tortured but consistent claims of historians and commentators over the last half century, Nixon and Reagan captured the political spirit of this troubled age because they spoke to the broad fears of millions of voters *without* appealing to racial resentments.

In a joint appearance at the National Negro Republican Assembly during his primary campaign in 1966 against fellow Republican George Christopher of San Francisco, Reagan was asked about his opposition to the Civil Rights Act of 1964. Christopher argued that

Goldwater's failing to support the act "did more harm than anything to the Republican Party, and we're still paying for that defeat. This situation still plagues the Republican Party, and unless we cast out this image, we're going to suffer defeat."

Reagan was furious. "I resent the implication that there is any bigotry in my nature," he replied. "Don't anyone ever imply I lack integrity. I will not stand silent and let anyone imply that—in this or any other group." According to biographer and journalist Lou Cannon, Reagan then "stalked" out of the meeting.

In his first campaign, the Gipper proved to be a confounding figure, a man who resisted the attempts of his opponents, and the media, to write him off as a right-winger from the Goldwater school of campaigning. As Matthew Dallek, who wrote a book on the 1966 gubernatorial race called, rightly, *The Right Moment: Ronald Reagan's First Victory and the Decisive Turning Point in American Politics,* noted: "In a clear departure from the gloomy defiance that had characterized Barry Goldwater's presidential campaign, and in a conscious attempt to distance himself from his earlier statements about communist hordes and totalitarian tyrannies, Reagan showed a sanguine disposition that emphasized the possibilities and glories of California life."

In his speech announcing his candidacy for governor, Reagan said: "California's problems are our problems. It won't matter if the sky is bigger and bluer out there if you can't see it for smog, and all our elbowroom and open space won't mean much if the unsolved problems are higher than the hills. Our problems are many, but our capacity for solving them is limitless."

Reagan's California campaign was about pitching the biggest tent possible. Like Eisenhower before him, Ronald Reagan knew that a conservative ideology worked best when married to a moderate temperament. Regardless of the undeserved contempt Ike received from movement conservatives, the fact is that he bent history by getting the GOP back into the Oval Office and appointing cabinet members who had more faith in the power of free markets than the idealistic experimentations of Washington politicians.

"I Like Ike" blended easily into Reagan's optimism. "I always wear the white hat," Reagan would tell staffers during his first term in the White House, and it was a strategy employed in 1966 to move past the crushing defeats of the last national election. Gone were the rough edges of Goldwater's 1964 bid; Reagan offered conservatism with a grin and geniality. And it wasn't an affectation. Reagan believed in the greatness of America because the country had been so good to him. That winning smile was more dangerous to American liberalism than any talking point dreamed up by a conservative think tank.

And like Ike, Reagan was practical.

"We do have the party glued together," Reagan wrote privately after winning the GOP nomination for governor, "if only we can keep some of the kooks quiet." He started to talk about a "Creative Society" of individual initiative.

Reagan's pragmatic conservatism worked with voters. Man and moment were made for each other. When Pat Brown joked that an actor had killed Lincoln, the Democratic incumbent struck exactly the wrong note. Reagan, for his part, stayed upbeat. "There isn't anything we can't do, and that includes solving the one overriding issue of this campaign . . . the issue besetting not only California, but also the nation . . . the issue that over-shadows and colors all others," Reagan said. "It is the issue of simple morality. Who among us doesn't feel concern for the deterioration of old standards, the abandonment of principles time-tested and proven in our climb from the swamp to the stars?"

Ronald Reagan won in a landslide, defeating Pat Brown by nearly a million votes.

The Reagan Revolution, though it was not yet called that, was under way.

The Johnsonian Great Society, centered as it was on government action, was to be confronted directly and explicitly in Reagan's California.

"The path we will chart is not an easy one," Reagan said in his gubernatorial inaugural address in 1967. "It demands much of those chosen to govern, but also from those who did the choosing. And let there be no mistake about this. We have come to a crossroad—a time of decision—and the path we follow turns away from any idea that government and those who serve it are omnipotent. It is a path impossible to follow unless we have faith in the collective wisdom and genius of the people. Along this path government will lead but not rule, listen but not lecture. It is the path of a Creative Society."

Looking back at 1966 from the perspective of 1981, a Pat Brown adviser told Lou Cannon: "Reagan was underestimated, and he still is. We tried to make him out a sinister figure, as Jimmy Carter did in 1980. It didn't work for us, and it didn't work in subsequent campaigns. Reagan has no harsh edge to him . . . is terribly pleasant, highly articulate and has a serious approach about politics. People like him, and we didn't understand that. We missed the human dimension of Ronald Reagan."

One wonders a generation later why the Republican Party has so totally forgotten the importance of Reagan's humanity and moderate temperament.

During Reagan's day it was Democrats who underestimated Reagan's personal appeal and missed so much more than that. Liberal critics also discounted his essential pragmatism, the same pragmatism, rooted in classically conservative principles, that had enabled him to run not as a candidate of darkness but of light.

There's no doubt that caricatures can be dangerous, but there are very few cases in history of a caricature doing more harm to a cause than what the left's caricature of Ronald Reagan did to liberalism from the mid-1960s onward. Winning the governorship was just the start. Once in Sacramento, Reagan spoke like a conservative and governed like a moderate. In those pre–*Roe v. Wade* days, he signed a liberal abortion law. He raised taxes to balance the budget when he had to. But he also took on a university system and a youth culture that for many Californians had become an emblem not of culture but of the counterculture. Hippies, Reagan remarked, as only Reagan could remark, "acted like Tarzan, looked like Jane, and smelled like Cheetah."

The possibility of seeking the presidency was always humming in the air around Reagan, and he was not shy about making a move toward the big prize less than two years into his governorship. In a sign that conservatives viewed Reagan's place in the firmament as an heir to Goldwater, political consultant Clifton White, late of the Goldwater insurgency, signed on to the Reagan presidential bid in 1968. White's task was a lot like his work earlier in the decade: take a candidate many professionals discount and propel him to the top of the ticket by appealing to individual delegates and delegations rather than the traditional party leadership.

Reagan in '68 was a distant but not unrealistic hope. Lou Cannon, then covering Reagan in California, called the most optimistic Reaganauts the "Reagan Presidentialists," supporters who, along with Clif White, believed that Reagan might be able to win over enough Southern backers to create an open convention by denying Richard Nixon a first-ballot victory. After that, perhaps Reagan's Hollywood magic could win over even more delegates fearing yet another Nixon loss. Backers created campaign literature proclaiming "No Problem Is Too Big for Reagan"—a foreshadowing of his ultimate national reputation. His time had not yet arrived, however.

Reagan's win in '66 had come in a big Republican year—forty-seven House seats and three Senate gains. The vote was a clear rebuke to President Johnson, the man who had seemed so invincible only two years earlier, when he buried Goldwater in the general election. The riots, following closely on the heels of civil rights legislation, the growing war in Vietnam, the cultural chaos described above, and a rising disenchantment with massive domestic Great Society programs had combined to curtail Johnson's influence in an astonishingly short period of time.

The reign of Johnsonian liberalism, which was really an attempt by the old Texas New Dealer to continue FDR's transformation of American life, was to be brief. Hugh Sidey of *Time* once watched Johnson caress the contours of a bust of FDR and listen to the president muse about Roosevelt's courage and strength. But the bust was not a talisman, or, if it was, its magic was fleeting, fading fast in the face of the conservative counterrevolution of 1966.

* * *

It was a correction led not only by Reagan but by Richard Nixon, who had used his new base as a high-priced New York lawyer to campaign for House, Senate, and gubernatorial candidates in the off-year race. Nixon had become a neighbor of Nelson Rockefeller's on Fifth Avenue, near the scene of his 1960 parlay with the New York governor over the GOP platform on the eve of the general election campaign against JFK. From his perch as a law partner of John Mitchell's, Nixon had returned to the political vineyard, campaigning tirelessly around the country.

Nixon's goal had been to elect fellow Republicans and to try to mend his image as a perennial loser, no small task after 1960 and a disastrous run for governor of California in 1962 which ended in a November 7 press conference where all of the losing candidate's worst qualities came tumbling out at once. Resentment, anger, and self-pity were the emotions that poured out of Richard Nixon's mouth to a hostile press corps. He ended the doomed campaign by saying, "You don't have Nixon to kick around any more because, gentlemen, this is my last press conference."

Political obituaries flooded the press over the following week. With characteristic élan, Teddy White was to invoke Charles Dickens to describe Nixon's political status at the beginning of 1963, comparing the former vice president, defeated presidential nominee, and defeated gubernatorial candidate to Ebenezer Scrooge's partner, Jacob Marley: "Marley was dead: to begin with. There is no doubt whatever about that. The register of his burial was signed by the clergyman, the clerk, the undertaker, and the chief mourner. . . . Old Marley was as dead as a door-nail." Except, like Marley on that fateful Christmas Eve, Nixon wasn't quite in the ground yet.

Not by a long shot.

5

The Lift of a Driving Dream

"Bring Us Together."
—*A sign in a Nixon campaign crowd in Ohio, 1968*

"We cannot learn from one another until we stop shouting at one another—until we speak quietly enough so that our words can be heard as well as our voices."
—*Richard Nixon, January 20, 1969*

WHEN RICHARD NIXON WAS WEIGHING WHETHER TO SEEK the presidency yet again in 1968, his older daughter may have captured the situation best. After Julie, his younger daughter, told him, "You have to do it for the country," Tricia cut closer to the heart of the matter.

"If you don't run, Daddy," she said, "you really will have nothing to live for."

Nixon also sought counsel from Billy Graham. At Bebe Rebozo's Key Biscayne retreat, the man who lost to Kennedy by less than half of one percent spent hours with the great evangelical preacher during the last days of 1967. Graham read aloud from the first and second chapters of Paul's epistle to the Romans. As the preacher was packing to leave, Nixon asked him what the decision ought to be.

"Well, what is your conclusion?" Nixon said.

"Dick, I think you should run," Graham replied. "If you don't you will always wonder whether you could have won or not. You are the best prepared man in the United States to be President."

As he was leaving the Florida retreat, Billy Graham took on the role of a prophet: "I think it is your destiny to be President."

In Nixon, Billy Graham's inspired message reached willing ears. Nixon decided to roll the dice on destiny, announcing at his first gathering of reporters in New Hampshire: "Gentlemen, this is *not* my last press conference."

What lay behind the resurrection of Richard Nixon in 1968? Not a run to the right. The Old Nixon ran campaigns fueled by resentment and Red-baiting. The New Nixon's path to political redemption, if there was to be a path, would be about appealing to wide audiences rather than narrow ones. Ray Price, a Nixon adviser, would say that his boss was most successful when he would be "neither a conservative nor a liberal [but] a centrist." Like Reagan in California, Nixon was learning a timeless American truth. We like leaders who point us toward the light, not leaders who try to make us afraid of the dark. The New Nixon of '66 and, soon, of '68 was a man who talked of what he called the "lift of a driving dream."

Republicans were ready to give *that* Nixon, the new one, one more shot. Reagan made a convention run for the nomination, but the Nixon forces had already put away challenges from Rockefeller and Michigan's George Romney and so Reagan's bid was more quixotic than real.

What was undeniably real was a Miami Beach convention that

seemed to have learned the negative lessons that flowed out of Goldwater's "extremism" rant in San Francisco's Cow Palace during their 1964 conclave. The GOP of 1968 appeared to have more in common with the optimism of Reagan's California than with the hard-edged idealism of the GOP convention held in the Golden State four years earlier.

Most strikingly, that lesson seemed to be absorbed the most by Goldwater himself. In an address to the convention in Miami, the 1964 standard-bearer struck different notes than he had four years earlier.

"We are not here to accuse and we are not here to divide," Barry Goldwater told the delegates. "The target is not to be found in this Convention Hall in Miami; it is not to be found in the Republican Party anywhere." Goldwater added: "We are here to deliver a message to the future and to find a meaning for today. We are not here to moan about yesterday. We can learn from yesterdays but we cannot live them nor go back to them."

Liberals have long been reluctant to give Richard Nixon his due. History books have long portrayed him as a political hack who used whatever means necessary—including race-baiting—to get to the top. That is, of course, no more fair than judging LBJ exclusively on his racist comments, stolen elections, and segregationist past. Peeling away years of Nixon hatred, though, lets us see that the campaign that finally brought him the prize he had sought so long was in reality more Clintonian than draconian.

The New Nixon spoke of common concerns. There was an emerging voice out there, he said, "different from the old voices, the voices of hatred, the voices of dissension, the voices of riot and revolution. What is happening is that the Forgotten Americans, those who did not indulge in violence, those who did not break the law, people who pay their taxes and go to work, people who send their children to school, who go to their churches, people who are not haters, people who love this country, and because they love this country are angry about what has happened to America, the Forgotten Americans, I call them . . . they cover all spectrums, they are laborers and they are managers, and they are white people and they are black people . . . who cry out . . . 'that is enough, let's get some new leadership.'"

The *Charlotte Observer*, reporting on a Nixon Southern stop, realized that Nixon's "Southern Strategy" was more a "Suburban Strategy." Speaking to Southerners, the *Observer* wrote, Nixon drew on "Norman Rockwell, *Reader's Digest*, and the lighter side of Sinclair Lewis. [Nixon] crossed no Mason-Dixon lines of the mind and . . . certainly didn't try to out-Wallace George Wallace. . . . He was speaking to the 45-year-old man with the mortgage, the housewife taking a job so the last child can go to college, and all the nonviolent fed-up. . . . Nixon's paradise is not one achieved without sacrifice. But it is the sacrifice for the kids, for the house in the suburbs, of good old All-American hard work, not the sacrifice of tax money for more federal programs or of old attitudes." He was speaking to my father, a man who woke up early in the suburbs of Atlanta and drove to work while his wife and three children still lay in bed, sleeping in a neighborhood not as safe or sheltered or secure from upheaval as it had been a few years earlier. Richard Nixon's brand of law and order had more to do with policing inner city neighborhoods. It was about the moderate Republican grabbing the torch from William F. Buckley and standing athwart history yelling stop! Pushing back at the radicalism of 1968 and praying that someone, anyone, could bring an end to the most culturally chaotic year since the Civil War ended a century earlier.

Nixon was running this campaign in the worst of years, a time of serial crisis and bloodshed. There was Vietnam, the Tet Offensive in January, the My Lai massacre in mid-March, LBJ's stunning farewell from politics at the end of that same month, Martin Luther King, Jr.'s, assassination four days later on April 4, Robert Francis Kennedy's death in June, the chaos of Chicago at the end of the summer, and thousands of lesser societal shocks that made Americans believe their country was cracking at its core. The nation was no longer spinning out of control. It *was* out of control, and her noblest sons were paying the price by falling to the bullets of assassins.

Despite the contempt liberals felt for Richard Nixon from the moment they first became aware of the Orange County congressman, many on the left focused their rage more on the Democratic nominee that year, Hubert Humphrey. That anger at the old Democratic establishment poured out into the streets of Chicago during the Democratic convention, causing incalculable damage to the Democrats. The unhinged nature of radical rage was neatly summed up by the legendary Hunter S. Thompson, whose hatred for Richard Nixon was rivaled only by his contempt for Hubert Humphrey.

"There is no way to grasp what a shallow, contemptible and hopelessly dishonest old hack Hubert Humphrey is," Thompson wrote, "until you've followed him around for a while." Exactly how such a fundamentally decent man (who took up the cause of civil rights decades before most Democrats dared to follow) became an enemy of the left seems unfathomable decades later. It speaks to the radical, even irrational nature of the times.

White anger and uncertainty over civil rights was a national, not a regional, issue, but Nixon knew that George Wallace's independent candidacy could hurt most in the South, where Strom Thurmond's Dixiecrats had done well just two decades before. In *The Selling of the President 1968,* the journalist Joe McGinniss reports a long scene of Nixon filming ads in October to run in the closing weeks of the race. One ad is aimed at Southerners who probably sympathized with Thurmond in '48 and had voted for Goldwater in '64 but who weren't so sure about Nixon, whose record on civil rights was comparatively progressive.

Here is Nixon's message, which he spoke into a camera without a TelePrompTer:

There's been a lot of double-talk about the role of the South in the campaign of nineteen sixty-eight, and I think it's time for some straight talk. If there were a straight-up-and-down vote as to whether the people of the South wanted to continue in office those that have helped to make the policies of the last four years, in other words, whether they're for Hubert Humphrey for President, the vote would be three to one against him. Only if that vote divides is it possible for Hubert Humphrey to even have a chance to be elected the next President of the United States. And so I say, don't play their game. Don't divide your vote. Vote for the team, the only team that can provide the new leadership that America needs, the Nixon-Agnew team. And I pledge to you that we will restore law and order in this country, we will bring peace abroad, and we will restore respect for America all

over the world. And we will provide that prosperity without war,
and progress without inflation that every American wants.

Here, Nixon again makes liars of those critics who seek to paint him as the diabolical race-baiter who preyed on white racists' fears to win elections. Nixon's plea to Southern conservatives was the same he made to Northeast moderates and West Coast independents. America was out of control, a quiet majority was rising, and the time had come to fight back against those who weren't playing by the rules.

From Edmund Burke to the conservative philosopher Russell Kirk to William F. Buckley, conservatism has been about the preservation of order and the elevation of eternal truths over political trends "arrived at yesterday at the voting booth." That conservative streak also carried with it a realistic sense of humanity's vices and virtues and a pragmatic understanding of just how far public opinion could be bent before voters kicked you out of office. Without the maintenance of order—government's first and probably most significant function—then nothing else is possible. Without order we descend rapidly into Thomas Hobbes's war of all against all. There is a reason why those who drafted our Constitution saw as their top order of business, after establishing justice, insuring our "domestic Tranquility."

Domestic tranquility was not a phrase that rolled easily off the tongues of many Americans in 1968. In that bleak chapter of American history, chaos, not order, was the default setting for American society. Three British journalists tellingly entitled an epic chronicle of the year *An American Melodrama*. By the time the voters went to the polls in November 1968 they were exhausted by history and wanted, if not a holiday, at least a sense that *somebody* could be counted on to calm the surging waters. With the Democratic Party at war with itself, Richard Nixon worked frantically in the final weeks to avoid another heartbreaking loss by the narrowest of margins.

On the last flight of the campaign, from Los Angeles to Newark, Nixon noticed a poster in the cabin emblazoned with the now familiar slogan "Nixon's the One."

"I hope it's right," the candidate remarked, before settling in for the long trip east.

It was, if barely. Conservatism in the classic sense carried the day in 1968 but because of George Wallace's third-party bid, Nixon won the presidency with just 43 percent of the vote, narrowly defeating the Democrats' Humphrey. As Nixon remarked after the election, he knew from 1960 what it was like to be on the losing side of such a close race, and winning was "a lot more fun."

The Nixon who won the presidency in 1968 ignored the old orthodoxies within the GOP. The anticommunist crusader in him embraced global engagement and free trade, a shift away from earlier Republican positions that included isolationism and support for protective tariffs.

"We seek an open world—open to ideas, open to the exchange of goods and people—a world in which no people, great or small, will live in angry isolation," said Nixon. Nixon's GOP was a different, more modern party than the one that had twice nominated Thomas Dewey.

Nixon understood the great forces of change. "There certainly is a new Nixon," the candidate remarked during the campaign. "I realize, too, that as a man gets older he learns something. If I haven't learned something I am not worth anything in public life. We live in a new world. Half the nations in the world were born since World War II. Half the people living in the world today were born since World War II. The problems are different. . . . I think I have some ideas as to how we can promote peace, ideas that are different from what they were eight years ago, not because I have changed but because the problems have changed." One wonders how today's Republican Party would embrace such change in their standard-bearer. Considering that the base's positions on a variety of issues from taxes to immigration to guns have moved far to the right of even Ronald Reagan, it remains an open question whether the GOP in its current state is pragmatic enough to tack with the political winds that whirl around it today.

Among the many tragedies of Richard Milhous Nixon was the failure of the better angels of his nature to win out over the darker impulses of his political soul. For be sure of this: Nixon had those better angels. He was not the evil incarnate that liberals feared and loathed for so long. He was a man who wrestled with his demons while struggling to bring order to a disordered nation and find an end to a tragic war.

Taking stock of the Nixon who finally repeated the words of the oath of office from Chief Justice Earl Warren on January 20, 1969, makes Nixon's later fall all the more poignant. At last at the very top of the greasy pole, at last on equal footing with the great Eisenhower, at last politically redeemed from his defeats in 1960 and 1962, the boy from Whittier dreamed of greatness. And the man whose early career in politics was defined by division gave a first inaugural address that was a model of warmth and unity.

"The simple things are the ones most needed today if we are to surmount what divides us, and cement what unites us," Nixon said that day on the East Front of the Capitol. "To lower our voices would be a simple thing. In these difficult years, America has suffered from a fever of words; from inflated rhetoric that promises more than it can deliver; from angry rhetoric that fans discontents into hatreds; from bombastic rhetoric that postures instead of persuading."

Nixon's tone and message were inclusive.

"For its part, government will listen," he said. "We will strive to listen in new ways—to the voices of quiet anguish, the voices that speak without words, the voices of the heart—to the injured voices, the anxious voices, the voices that have despaired of being heard. Those who have been left out, we will try to bring in. Those left behind, we will help to catch up. For all of our people, we will set as our goal the decent order that makes progress possible and our lives secure."

Within the first year of his presidency Nixon tapped into a broad frustration on the part of many Americans that their voices in the public square had been drowned out by radicals and ignored by elitists. As Garry Wills wrote in *National Review* the day after Nixon's victory, "The liberal Eastern establishment found that it was not needed on Election Day—which made its leaders take a second look at the forgotten American . . . paying the bill for progress, who found its values mocked by the spokesmen of that progress." Nixon was now speaking to Wills's "forgotten American."

"Let historians not record that when America was the most powerful nation in the world we passed on the other side of the road and allowed the last hopes for peace and freedom of millions of people to be suffocated by the forces of totalitarianism," Nixon said in a November 1969 speech. "And so tonight—to you, the great silent majority of my fellow Americans—I ask for your support."

The reaction was swift and transforming: the Silent Majority broke its silence, and Nixon released a photograph of himself and White House chief of staff H. R. "Bob" Haldeman surrounded by stacks and stacks of letters and telegrams of support of the speech in the Oval Office. It was classic Nixon, the man whose political career was saved in 1952 when Ike was flooded by telegrams of support for his vice presidential pick following the "Checkers Speech," in which Nixon addressed accusations of having inappropriate access to a "secret fund," successfully securing his place on the national ticket.

Shortly after this appeal to the Silent Majority, Vice President Spiro Agnew went to Des Moines, Iowa, to offer a critique of the television-news establishment. In the spirit of Sidney Lumet's *Network*, Agnew urged Americans to get mad as hell and not take it anymore. Agnew said: "A raised eyebrow, an inflection of the voice, a caustic remark dropped in the middle of a broadcast can raise doubts in a million minds about the veracity of a public official or the wisdom of a Government policy. One Federal Communications Commissioner considers the powers of the networks equal to that of local, state, and Federal Governments all combined. Certainly it represents a concentration of power over American public opinion unknown in history."

Agnew pressed the point. "Now what do Americans know of the men who wield this power? Of the men who produce and direct the network news, the nation knows practically nothing. Of the commentators, most Americans know little other than that they reflect an urbane and assured presence seemingly well-informed on every important matter. We do know that to a man these commentators and producers live and work in the geographical and intellectual confines of Washington, D.C., or New York City, the latter of which James Reston terms the most unrepresentative community in the entire United States. Both communities bask in their own provincialism, their own parochialism."

The same failed candidate who spent his "final press conference" striking back at reporters was now running a White House that seemed to serve as a kind of rolling referendum on the liberal establishment that had first inspired Buckley to rebel against the prevailing intellectual and political order. In a private White House meeting in 1969, former President Johnson helpfully advised Nixon to think of the press as a bipartisan hater.

"He felt that newspapermen are just naturally vicious and are not happy unless they are attacking somebody," Nixon recalled LBJ saying.

How much of the Nixon critique was genuinely conservative and how much was rhetorical is a question historians will long debate, for Nixon governed far, far differently than a Goldwater would have.

On domestic policy, Nixon was no conservative.

"Don't promise more than we can do," he advised his cabinet. "But do more than we can promise." He created the Environmental Protection Agency and the Occupational Safety and Health Administration; he proposed extensive health care reform; he argued for a guaranteed minimum income plan for the poor. Interestingly, Nixon, a creature of government since his election to Congress in 1946, never fully absorbed the free enterprise ethos that so many other Republicans embodied. Perhaps that is why he championed wage and price controls that conservatives like myself still find to be an economic abomination forty years later. Asking what the public sector might be able to do to solve a problem came naturally to Nixon despite his occasional anti-Washington rhetoric. One of his signature achievements was "revenue sharing," where the federal government kept tax rates in place but gave local and state authorities a proportion of revenue to spend. "The country recognizes the need for change," Nixon told his first meeting of the new Urban Affairs Council, "and we don't want the record written that we were too cautious."

On foreign policy, the opening to China and the work toward détente with the Soviets were hallmarks of an administration that thought big and acted big.

The problem, of course, was that beneath the truly magisterial vision Nixon brought to the presidency lay a persistent smallness fed by tough-guy staffers who put swagger above smarts. Most large organizations embrace a culture that reflects its leader, and Richard Nixon made it all possible, creating a climate of paranoia amid some of the great moments in modern presidential history.

6

Acid, Amnesty, and Abortion

"You fellows just don't know McGovern—you think he's an evil man. He is just the stupidest man there ever was."
—*Democratic National Committee chairman Robert Strauss*

EVEN LYNDON JOHNSON WAS SKEPTICAL ABOUT HIS PARTY'S 1972 presidential nominee. After George McGovern won the top spot on the ticket at the Democratic National Convention, Richard Nixon called LBJ in Texas. "Let me just read you a letter, Mr. President," Johnson told Nixon. "This is the standard reply I'm sending out to Democrats who write me about what they should do because they're so disenchanted with McGovern. It says that because of the honor I have been given by my party over forty years, I am going to support the Democratic ticket at all levels. However, I go on to say— and no one will fail to catch this—that I have always taken the position that what an individual does in a presidential campaign is a matter of conscience, and I'm not going to interfere with that decision. Now what do you think of that?"

"I can only say that I'm very grateful, Mr. President," Nixon replied.

Johnson's coolness toward McGovern was but a hint of the Nixon landslide to come. McGovern represented what came to be known as "acid, amnesty, and abortion"; his campaign was the nadir of the extreme liberalism that had become such a debilitating force in Democratic presidential politics.

Richard Nixon called his supporters the "New Majority"—a coalition of voters that included FDR Democrats who would still vote the party line in state and local elections but jump to the GOP when national races were involved. It is the unenviable position that the current Republican Party now finds itself in, owning the U.S. House, 60 percent of governorships, and the majority of state legislatures while still managing to lose five of the last six popular votes for president. In 1972, the safest, most practical vote in the presidential race seemed to be Richard Nixon. He played to the pragmatism of his time by making the election about competence instead of ideology.

"The choice in this election is not between radical change and no change," Nixon said in accepting renomination in 1972. "The choice in this election is between change that works and change that won't work."

For Nixon, 1972 offered a remarkable opportunity. With the national Democratic Party in a state of near anarchy after the chaos of Chicago in 1968 and Miami in 1972, the nomination of George McGovern offered an all too rare opening for a real realignment. The American center was, it seemed, no longer divided fairly evenly between Democrats and Republicans. By offering moderation in a time of radicalism, Nixon and the GOP had the chance to build that New Majority.

Watching McGovern win the nomination, Nixon was exuberant— or as exuberant as Nixon could get. McGovern, Nixon recalled, "had consciously abandoned conservative and moderate Democrats; and the ethnic groups, traditionally a Democratic blue chip, could find in him nothing of the hearty patriotism and pride that they had looked for in their party in the past."

Reflecting privately on McGovern, Nixon told an adviser, "The Eastern Establishment media finally has a candidate who almost totally shares their views.... *The New York Times, The Washington Post, Time, Newsweek,* and the three television networks ... their editorial bias comes down on the side of amnesty, pot, abortion, confiscation of wealth (unless it is theirs), massive increases in welfare, unilateral disarmament, reduction of their defenses, and surrender in Vietnam."

A vote for Nixon from traditional Democrats might prove the first step toward a more permanent union with the Republicans, or with Nixonian political successors. Officials in the president's reelection campaign were told to attack "McGovernites," not "Democrats."

As Nixon speechwriter Pat Buchanan described it, the New Majority was formed when "Nixon sliced off from FDR's New Deal coalition Northern Catholics and ethnics—Irish, Italians, Poles, East Europeans—and Southern Christian conservatives. Where FDR and Woodrow Wilson had won all 11 Southern States six times, Nixon swept them all in '72. And where Nixon won only 22 percent of the Catholic vote against JFK, he won 55 percent against George McGovern in 1972."

The party was changing. Flying eastward on Election Day, Nixon took time to sit down with Teddy White. He might just have "shifted allegiances" this year, Nixon told the old campaign chronicler. "Just think of the shift in the South," said Nixon. It wasn't race that had done it—no, it wasn't that. "You know what did it? Patriotism, not racism." As White characterized the rest of Nixon's points, "Not only the South was shifting, but others—workingmen and Catholics, too. The Republican Party used to be a WASP party, he recalled, and he used to talk about it in the old days with Len Hall, who came from Nassau County. Len understood. You used to go to a Republican dinner in those days and there wouldn't be an Irishman or an Italian or a Jew there. If you could shift those allegiances permanently, then this landslide might mean something."

A self-consciously prototypical member of the postwar middle class, Nixon grasped the demographic realities of his time. No party could be successful nationally by being either locked into extremes or being totally dependent on a single ethnic group. If Republicans wanted to win consistently, they had to recognize and adapt to changing circumstances.

Nixon believed he could expand the base of his party by seeking to rally people of different backgrounds around common concerns about declining standards.

"I was ready to take a stand on . . . social and cultural issues; I was anxious to defend the 'square' virtues," Nixon recalled. "In some cases—such as opposing the legalization of marijuana and the provision of federal funds for abortions, and in identifying myself with unabashed patriotism—I knew I would be standing against the prevailing social winds, and that would cause tension. But I thought that at least someone in high office would be standing up for what he believed." As he had since his first campaign in 1946, Richard Nixon had defined himself by the enemies he kept. The "Pink Lady" (Helen Gahagan Douglas) would have been comfortable in George McGovern's Democratic Party, Nixon surely thought. And like Reagan, both Old and New Nixon alike knew there was much to be gained across America by running against Eastern elites.

Nixon knew a large majority vote would be required for him to effectively govern.

"We are seeking in this election something that no President has had since 1956, with the exception of President Johnson in '64 after his landslide, and that is a majority, because there was not a majority even in 1960 and of course there was not in 1968 because of third-party candidates," Nixon told reporters during a San Clemente press conference in late August 1972. "I think what we need now is a clear majority, a clear majority of the American people. That means a clear mandate, a mandate for what I have described as change that works, for progress. Because, when I see what has happened to, for example, revenue sharing, government reorganization, our health plan, our welfare reform, and all of our programs—there are 12 different bills on the environment that are still stuck in the mud of Senate and House controversy—when I see that, I think that the country needs to speak out."

Worries about the capacity of the Republican Party to adapt rapidly and thoroughly enough to make itself into something resembling the Democratic Party of FDR and Truman—and thus govern for several decades—led Nixon to consider the most radical of routes: creating a new party.

"As I began the new term," Nixon recalled in his memoirs, "I had a sense of urgency about the need to revitalize the Republican Party lest the New Majority slip away from us." Bob Dole was yielding—

reluctantly—the chairmanship of the Republican National Committee to George H. W. Bush, late of the United Nations after losing to Lloyd Bentsen in the 1970 Senate race in Texas. But Nixon was mulling something much larger: a scrambling of the partisan assumptions that had more or less shaped American politics since the nomination of Abraham Lincoln for president in Chicago in 1860. Something had to be done to shake up the party since Nixon's forty-nine-state victory had done nothing to move Republicans toward the majority on Capitol Hill. In fact, Senate Republicans had swum against the political tide and somehow managed to lose two seats.

What about a new and different operation? The option was a live one in Nixon's White House for a time. "We even deliberated for several days about starting a new party," Nixon said. "There was no question that the party had ability—it had some of the most able and principled men and women in public life. It seemed to me that what we most lacked was the ability to *think* like a majority party, to take risks, to exhibit the kind of confidence the Democrats had because of their sheer numbers."

On December 1, 1972, the prospect of a new party that would nominate Treasury Secretary John Connally, a Democrat-turned-Republican, for president in 1976 came up in a conversation between Nixon and his closest advisers, Bob Haldeman and John Ehrlichman. A Haldeman diary entry records the episode:

The "Connally for President" discussion led to a general discussion of forming a new party. E [Ehrlichman] raising the idea that this is our only chance, in the next 60 days or so, and that we should give some thought to it on the basis that you use the Republican Party as a base, but add to it the New Majority. Use

Connally as the focal point candidate, but that the P has to take
the lead. The P was intrigued with this as a possibility, recogniz-
ing that you can never really go with the P's party into a major-
ity and that the only hope probably is to do a new party. The
question is whether it can be done and whether we really want
to make the effort.

Haldeman and Connally covered the same ground a few weeks
later. The old Texas pol was eager to run for president but skeptical
that it could be done without the support of the Republican Party.

"Had a long session with Connally and the whole question of the
new party and Connally's going for the presidency," Haldeman
wrote, "and it's clear that Connally is ready to run, but not totally
convinced that we can do it by building a new party. The third-party
route just isn't workable, and there's no point in trying it. He does
feel that we could do something in the way of re-establishing the
Republican Party in a different way, with a new name, such as the
Republican Independent Party. It would clearly put a new cast on it,
but not lose the base that we have now, which Connally feels is indis-
pensable."

Why was Nixon—the politician who by now had received the most
votes in the history of the GOP—willing to even consider undoing
his own party? Such a move would have required a new coalition
that would have inevitably forced some existing elements of the coalition out. Presumably Nixon was thinking that a fiscally responsible, moderately hawkish, and socially tolerant party could attract

enough swing voters and independents to join with traditional Republicans to create an actual New Majority.

Nothing came of the musings, and soon enough Watergate would sweep away everything in its path. Yet it was Richard Nixon who saw a great political truth that has yet to be effectively acted upon: that millions of Americans, silent and otherwise, feel the traditional two-party system that has monopolized American politics for over 150 years serves ideologues and special interests more than the majority that elects presidents.

Basking in the glow of his historic win, Nixon hoped his reelection had cemented the cultural counterrevolution that began in 1966 and led America into a new conservative epoch.

"We have passed through a very great spiritual crisis in this country," the president told *The Washington Star* in November 1972. "The average American is just like the child in the family. You give him some responsibility and he is going to amount to something.... Pamper him and cater to him too much, you are going to make him soft, spoiled and eventually a very weak individual."

So brilliant and shrewd in so many ways, the same politician who fought his way onto Eisenhower's ticket in 1952 managed to stay by Ike's side for the next eight years, even when Eisenhower wanted him gone, and then engineered his own improbable comeback and remarkable landslide victory, then became the mastermind of his own doom.

The Watergate scandal inflicted intense damage on the GOP in 1974. A few months after Nixon's painful resignation, congressional

Republicans suffered a massive loss. Two years after their party's forty-nine-state landslide over George McGovern, the South Dakota senator's party controlled sixty-one seats to the GOP's thirty-eight. In the U.S. House, Democrats owned a massive advantage over Republicans, picking up fifty-one seats and controlling 291 seats while Republicans won only 144. The man who just two years earlier had considered abandoning the Republican Party in favor of a third way was now the cause of its collapse.

What is so surprising is how remarkably little lasting damage the Nixon scandals had on the Republican Party. Sure, 1974 was a disaster, but Jimmy Carter only narrowly defeated Gerald Ford two years later—and did so only by presenting himself as a pragmatic, sober, realistic figure. The Southern governor was no ideologue and knew that the lesson of 1968 and 1972 was that winning national elections required support from Nixon's Silent Majority.

Four decades later, Richard Nixon's political legacy remains as complicated as he was. To win national mandates required principled conservatism and a willingness to embrace different viewpoints; unflinching conviction is dramatic but less conducive to victory. In the turbulent times in which he ran, victory went to the careful rather than to the crusader.

At Nixon's funeral in 1994, President Bill Clinton remarked that Richard Nixon was like his father, while Bob Dole broke down as he eulogized another striving son of the America whose power base was formed far beyond Manhattan and Cambridge. The second half of the twentieth century would one day come to be known as the Age of Nixon, the Senate majority leader from Kansas said.

Whether or not that proves to be the case, the thirty-seventh president of the United States surely did this much: he taught Republicans how to win national elections in times that are far from conservative and how to govern from the center when that provides Republicans the only path forward to victory. His demons got the better of him, but his example gave Republicans a playbook, one they would employ to get the better of Democrats for nearly twenty years after that last lonely wave from the steps of Marine One on the South Lawn of the White House. Nixon waved good-bye to us on that grim August day, but not to a Republican presidential majority. Even the worst scandal in presidential history could not stop the lift of a driving dream for a party that had finally learned how to tack with the wind and would now begin their move toward the majority.

7

The Dream Is Still with Us

"I believe the Republican Party represents basically the
thinking of the people of this country, if we can get that
message across to the people. I'm going to try to do that."
—*Ronald Reagan, 1974*

"You got me out, you sons of bitches. Now get
off your ass."
—*Vice President Nelson Rockefeller,*
to Southern Republicans after he withdrew from consideration
as Gerald Ford's 1976 running mate

IT WAS NOVEMBER 1975, JUST FIFTEEN MONTHS AFTER RICH-
ard Nixon's resignation and Gerald Ford's ascendancy to president,
when Ronald Reagan arrived at the National Press Club in Washington to announce his own candidacy for the Republican nomination. "We, as a people, aren't happy if we are not moving forward,"
Reagan said. "A nation that is growing and thriving is one which
will solve its problems. We must offer progress instead of stagnation;
the truth instead of promises; hope and faith instead of defeatism
and despair. Then, I am sure, the people will make those decisions

which will restore confidence in our way of life and release that energy that is the American spirit."

Classic Reagan—and that's what had the Ford White House worried. The incumbent's best hope seemed based less on the president's own strengths and more on the challenger's alleged weaknesses as a Goldwater ideologue with a vacant smile. In September 1975 a Ford adviser reported to Ford aides Dick Cheney and Don Rumsfeld on a conversation with former president Nixon at San Clemente. "RN feels that Ronald Reagan is a lightweight," said the adviser, "and not someone to be considered seriously or feared in terms of a challenge for the nomination."

Like most of Reagan's political opponents before and after the 1976 campaign, Ford's inner circle made the mistake of underestimating the greatest Republican politician since Lincoln. In a political memo sent to the president, an adviser wrote, "Regardless of whether or not Governor Reagan wins any primaries, President Ford will be by far the stronger candidate for the Republican Party in a general election, and to nominate Governor Reagan would be a repetition of 1964." In another memo, an adviser told White House press secretary Ron Nessen: "His general ignorance of national affairs—assuming it continues—will make President Ford look better and better every day. Of course, this does not mean we don't have to work hard. If we blunder, Reagan could be a serious threat."

Ford himself sensed that Reagan was going to be formidable. That was a term that had seldom attached itself to the Michigan politician over his three decades in public office.

"Gerry Ford is so dumb he can't fart and chew gum at the same time," Lyndon Johnson had said of the Republican minority leader despite the fact Ford voted for LBJ's civil rights bills. Bob Haldeman suggested that his boss ultimately selected Ford to replace Spiro Agnew because Nixon believed House members who had served with the minority leader for nearly three decades would be so aware of his shortcomings that they would never elevate him to the presidency by impeaching Nixon. And a cursory look at his long tenure in Congress shows that Jerry Ford never once drafted a piece of major legislation that became law.

But often the tides of history move in ways that even the most brilliant tacticians cannot predict. When on July 24, 1974, the U.S. Supreme Court ruled that Richard Nixon would be required to turn over the Watergate tapes, the thirty-seventh president knew that he would soon be impeached and face criminal prosecution. His attorney general, John Mitchell, told a panicked Nixon that the best he could do is strike a deal with Ford and resign immediately. So Nixon went hat in hand to a man whom he had little use for since they first started working together in Congress in 1948.

Nixon sent White House chief of staff Alexander Haig to Ford with an offer to resign the presidency immediately in return for a full pardon. Ford, a man of unquestioned integrity, agonized over the decision with his wife and closest advisers before rejecting the deal outright. While the vice president believed a pardon was in the best interest of the country, he also refused to be part of any deal that would elevate him into the Oval Office while casting a shadow over his character. If Ford were to grant the pardon, he would make that decision himself after, not before, moving into the White House. With his escape route blocked by Ford's stubborn morality, Nixon was eventually forced to resign before Congress threw him out on their own.

On Friday, August 9, 1974, Richard Nixon resigned from office and Jerry Ford was sworn in as thirty-eighth president of the United States by Chief Justice Warren Burger in a hastily arranged ceremony in the East Room of the White House. Ford told the small crowd assembled, "I am acutely aware that you have not elected me as your president by your ballots, and so I ask you to confirm me as your president with your prayers."

Ford reminded shocked Americans watching on TV and listening on radio that, despite the partisan warfare that had ripped Washington apart over the past decade, he was a moderate with an abundance of friends on both sides of the aisle. He also let them know that better days were ahead.

"My fellow Americans, our long national nightmare is over. Our Constitution works; our great Republic is a government of laws and not of men. Here, the people rule. But there is a higher Power, by whatever name we honor Him, who ordains not only righteousness but love, not only justice, but mercy. . . . Let us restore the golden rule to our political process, and let brotherly love purge our hearts of suspicion and hate."

Ford seemed to be everything that Richard Nixon was not—an honest man who possessed the kind of simple Midwest values that had carried America through a great depression and world war. Ford was a moderate domestically, an interventionist globally, and a conservative fiscally by the standards of his day. But soon after his swearing-in ceremony, Gerald Ford would anger conservatives by selecting the liberal New York governor Nelson Rockefeller as his vice president and would outrage most Americans by granting Nixon a full pardon. The outcry was immediate. *The Washington Post*'s Bob Woodward and Carl Bernstein, among others, suggested that a corrupt bargain with Nixon lay at the heart of the pardon. And *The New York Times* editorialized that the Nixon pardon was "a profoundly unwise, divisive and unjust act" that destroyed the new president's "credibility as a man of judgment, candor and competence."

Confident in his own skin and certain that his character remained intact, Jerry Ford did something that no president had done since Abraham Lincoln. He went before Congress and testified under oath as to the reasons why he granted the controversial pardon. Congress, the voters, and the national press would remain harshly critical of Ford, but history would prove the good and decent man from Grand Rapids to be well ahead of his time. In 2001, Senator Ted Kennedy would present Ford the Profile in Courage Award at the John F. Kennedy Presidential Library and praise the former president for making a decision that he had once opposed. JFK's daughter also showered Ford with praise.

"For more than a quarter century, Gerald Ford proved to the people of Michigan, the Congress, and our nation that politics can be a noble profession," said Caroline Kennedy in presenting the Profile in Courage Award to the former president. "As President, he made a controversial decision of conscience to pardon former president Nixon and end the national trauma of Watergate. In doing so, he placed his love of country ahead of his own political future."

The kind judgment of history must have been a soothing balm to the aging ex-president, but in the fall of 1974, President Ford found himself besieged from all sides. Liberals were repelled by the pardon and conservatives were outraged by the thought of Nelson Rockefeller as vice president. A challenge from Ronald Reagan now seemed inevitable. Ford was a creature of the center who was comfortable playing the role of moderator and conciliator, whereas Reagan was a conservative who saw his political mission as drawing the center closer to his own views without alienating those he was wooing. It was a big, fundamental difference, and it's partly this difference that made Reagan Reagan. This trait also distinguishes him, fundamentally, from all too many Republicans today, who seem less interested in moving voters to their position than in planting an ideological flag in the ground and declaring all those not in lockstep insufficiently conservative, unpatriotic, or worse. This approach allows these political Pharisees to feel self-righteously superior to all others. But it is an approach that also guarantees an endless streak of electoral losses to the Republican Party these shortsighted amateurs claim to be helping with their ideological purges.

In 1975, Ronald Reagan was not interested in making a statement in support of conservatism. He was interested in winning. His first step was to call the sitting president of the United States and deliver the stunning news that a member of his own party would be challenging him for the nomination in 1976. That call, which Ford would dub the "challenge from the right," had come from Reagan on the afternoon of November 19.

"Hello, Mr. President," Reagan had said. "I am going to make an announcement, and I want to tell you about it ahead of time. I am going to run for President. I trust we can have a good contest, and I hope that it won't be divisive."

"Well, Governor, I'm very disappointed," Ford replied. "I'm sorry you're getting into this. I believe I've done a good job and that I can be elected. Regardless of your good intentions, your bid is bound to be divisive. It will take a lot of money, a lot of effort, and it will leave a lot of scars. It won't be helpful, no matter which of us wins the nomination."

"I don't think it will be divisive," Reagan said. "I don't think it will harm the party."

"Well, I think it will."

That was that. As Ford recalled, "Neither of us is the type of person to waste words, and we concluded the conversation quickly. I think he really believed that his candidacy wouldn't be divisive, but I knew he was wrong. How can you challenge an incumbent President of your own party and *not* be divisive?" Ford went on: "The challenge was serious."

It had been a long time coming. When Ford took over as president, he was immediately confronted with the task of naming a vice president. Asked about who should be chosen, Reagan took the opportunity to remind people that the conservatives remained the power base of the GOP. "I happen to believe that what is termed by many as the conservative philosophy is the basic Republican philosophy," Reagan said. "It is a libertarian philosophy, a belief in the individual freedom and the reduction of government. And so, obviously, I would feel that we were committed to the mandate of 1972, the philosophical mandate, that people handed down in such overwhelming numbers, if the President should choose someone representative of the Republican Party."

Was Nelson Rockefeller "representative of the Republican Party"? Reagan did not think so, and he had a point. In the fluid political calculus of the mid-1970s, the lesson of the postwar period was that centrists (Ike and Nixon) could win nationally, while more liberal Republicans (Rockefeller) or more conservative ones (Goldwater) could not. One thing was clear: by choosing Rockefeller, Ford was placing himself squarely in the centrist wing of the party, with a lean to the left.

Ford sensed possible trouble with Reagan, and so the president called the governor as Reagan's term in Sacramento wound down to explore Reagan's joining the Ford administration. According to Lou Cannon, two of the options floated by the president were the ambassadorship to the Court of St. James and secretary of transportation.

Reagan declined. He had another job on this mind: Ford's.

"Now, I hope and pray that this administration is successful," Reagan told Cannon. "And that would take care of '76. Because it's never—in my book—it's never been important who's in the White House, it's what's done. And that's what I mean about the mandate. Whatever may happen, I would like to feel that I can continue to be a voice in the Republican Party insuring that the party pursues the philosophy that I believe should be the Republican philosophy."

As there had been with Nixon in the aftermath of the '72 race, there was the briefest of flirtations about creating a new conservative party by pulling the right wings of both the GOP and the Democrats together. "There could be one of those moments in time, I don't know," Reagan said in the fall of 1974. "I see the statements of disaffection of people in both parties—the loss of confidence. And you wonder which is the easiest. Do you restore the confidence or do you change the name or something? I don't know. I really don't." Holmes Tuttle, one of Reagan's critical supporters in his Kitchen Cabinet of unofficial advisers, moved quickly to shut down the speculation. "You're a Republican and you're going to stay one," Tuttle told Reagan.

So he was.

"I am not starting a third party," Reagan said a few weeks later. "I do not believe the Republican Party is dead. I believe the Republican Party represents basically the thinking of the people of this country, if we can get that message across to the people. I'm going to try to do that."

At a meeting of conservatives in early 1975, now former governor Reagan continued the theme. "Is it a third party we need or is it a new and revitalized second party, raising a banner of no pale pastels but bold colors which make it unmistakably clear where we stand on all the issues troubling the people?"

Reagan understood what Nixon had wrought in 1972—a massive victory for Republicans that was rhetorically gentle and politically pragmatic. For all his gifts, Ford was not the seer Reagan was, and he kept bungling the Reagan relationship, once having Don Rumsfeld, the White House chief of staff, offer Reagan the Commerce Department.

Echoing Nixon's language, the more astute Reagan observed, "The '72 election gave us a new majority, a long-overdue realignment based not on party labels—but on basic philosophy," said Reagan. "The tragedy of Watergate and the traumatic experience of these past years since then has obscured the meaning of that '72 election. But the mandate registered by the people still remains. The people have not changed in philosophy."

The question facing GOP primary voters in 1976 was whether Ford or Reagan could best carry out that mandate. The president did well in early voting, putting Reagan on the defensive until the pivotal North Carolina primary, which saved Reagan's candidacy and convinced him to stay in the race until the convention in Kansas City.

The Ford campaign tried to do to Reagan what Pat Brown had tried and failed to do to him in California: paint the Gipper as a nuclear cowboy who couldn't be trusted with supreme authority. "When you vote Tuesday, remember: Governor Ronald Reagan couldn't start a war," said Ford ads. "President Ronald Reagan could." On the stump, Ford said, "There is no question in my mind whatsoever that I can be elected, and I have grave reservations, very serious doubts, that any other Republican candidate can be elected." He struck the same theme again later that same day: "We don't want a repetition of the debacle that took place in 1964. We want a ticket from the courthouse to the White House that can win for the kind of America that is good for all of us."

It was a brutal fight through the spring. On May 7, 1976, Barry Goldwater wrote Ford a letter of advice on Senate letterhead. "You are the President," Goldwater admonished Ford. "Do not stupe [*sic*] to arguing with another candidate. Your speeches are a little bit too long. Get a good speech that is short and use it and use it and use it. . . . You are not going to get the Reagan vote. These are the same people who got me the nomination and they will never swerve, but ninety per cent of them will vote for you for President, so get after middle America."

It was stunning advice from the same man who had famously used his own presidential campaign vilifying moderates and telling a rapturous convention crowd of conservatives that extremism was no vice.

On the eve of the convention President Ford had a narrow delegate lead, 1,093 to 1,030, with 1,130 needed for victory. Worries about the political hand-to-hand combat—which now featured James A. Baker III of Texas as a Ford delegate hunter—spread among Republicans. "This is a pitiful little party at best," a "prominent California Republican" told *Time*. "The fight is precluding us from any chance to win in November." The anonymous voice had a point. In the nation as a whole, self-identified Republicans numbered between 18 percent and 25 percent, versus 42 percent and 50 percent for the Democrats.

To assuage the right, Ford had prevailed on Vice President Rockefeller to disclaim any interest in the 1976 GOP nomination to be the president's running mate. The post was open.

"We just got the best news we've had in months," Dick Cheney told Ford. Reagan had made a play for ticket balancing—and for some much needed Pennsylvania delegates—by choosing Senator Richard Schweiker, a moderate-to-liberal Republican, as his running mate if he were to win the nomination.

It was a pragmatic move designed to change the terms of the convention, which at the moment was heading toward nominating Ford. Yet the gamble failed, in part because it drove Clarke Reed's Mississippi Republicans into the arms of the White House. In a close convention, everything mattered, and Reed's delegation went with Ford after Reagan seemed to jettison his convictions by naming a running mate from the Rockefeller wing of the party. The Mississippi margin proved crucial in securing the nomination for Ford.

Reagan's Schweiker maneuver may have cost the Gipper, but close students of Reagan's campaigns and administrations in California weren't entirely surprised by Reagan's pragmatic strategy.

Reagan would do what it took to win.

On the final night of the convention, President Ford accepted the nomination of his party—aside from his primary victories, his first political election outside the Fifth Congressional District of Michigan.

"We Republicans have had some tough competition," Ford told the delegates at Kemper Arena in Kansas City. "We not only preach the virtues of competition, we practice them. But tonight we come together not on a battlefield to conclude a cease-fire, but to join forces on a training field that has conditioned us all for the rugged contest ahead. Let me say this from the bottom of my heart: After the scrimmages of the past few months, it really feels good to have Ron Reagan on the same side of the line."

Then, in a gesture entirely characteristic of the personally gracious Gerald Ford, the president waved Nancy and Ronald Reagan down from their seats to join him and the rest of the GOP elite on the dais. Reagan had not addressed the convention; the war for delegates had been such that the Ford team had kept the challenger away from the big microphone.

Until now. Offered the last word at a convention where he had lost the nomination to a man whose views on foreign and domestic policy he found insufficiently conservative, Ronald Reagan spoke to a national audience in a way he had not since his famous "Rendezvous with Destiny" speech for Goldwater in the closing days of the 1964 campaign.

"I believe the Republican party has a platform that is a banner of bold, unmistakable colors with no pale pastel shades," said Reagan. "We have just heard a call to arms, based on that platform. And a call to us to really be successful in communicating and reveal to the American people the difference between this platform and the platform of the opposing party which is nothing but a revamp and a reissue and a rerunning of a late, late show of the thing that we have been hearing from them for the last 40 years. . . . This is our challenge and this is why we're here in this hall tonight. Better than we've ever done before, we've got to quit talking to each other and about each other and go out and communicate to the world that we may be fewer in numbers than we've ever been but we carry the message they're waiting for. We must go forth from here united, determined and what a great general said a few years ago is true: 'There is no substitute for victory.' "

The convention exploded with cheers as television tape from the evening showed Secretary of State Henry Kissinger shifting in his seat uncomfortably.

An astute observer of power, one can't help but wonder whether Dr. Kissinger sensed the future rise of Reagan in the moment. Many in the convention hall did that night as he did himself. The next morning, in an appearance before his supporters, the former California governor quoted a poet: "Lay me down and bleed a while. Though I am wounded, I am not slain. I shall rise and fight again." In a letter written after he got home to California from Kansas City, Reagan said, "We are at peace with ourselves and believe the Lord must have something else in mind for us to do."

As Ronald and Nancy Reagan made the long, quiet flight home to California after the crushing convention loss, Martin Anderson, an aide, approached the man who had now come up short in two presidential runs and asked Reagan to sign his convention ticket. Reagan obliged, writing, "We fought, we dreamed and the dream is still with us."

Four years later, Ronald Reagan would again reach for that dream. The third time would prove to be the charm.

8

A New Hope

"A recession is when your neighbor loses his job. A depression is when you lose yours. Recovery is when Jimmy Carter loses his."

—*Ronald Reagan, 1980*

THE FOUR YEARS BETWEEN REAGAN'S HEARTBREAKING LOSS in 1976 and his reemergence in the 1980 campaign were times that shook America's confidence in a way not experienced since the Great Depression a half century earlier. Unemployment shot up over 10 percent, inflation rose to 18 percent by the start of the campaign, interest rates topped 20 percent, and the Iranian government allowed Islamic radicals to kidnap and hold Americans hostage for 444 days. The United States of America suffered through a deep malaise, and many columnists and commentators suggested that America's greatest days lay in its past. Jimmy Carter was governing in grim times, and at times the Democratic president seemed to be overmatched by events, as well as for the position he held.

A Republican victory in 1980 certainly seemed to be within reach, but the start of the GOP primary that year was anything but smooth. The Republican field was packed, with Reagan being the presumed front-runner. The 1980 hopefuls included George H. W. Bush, Bob Dole, Howard Baker, Phil Crane, John Anderson, and John Connally, who was destined to spend a Texas-sized fortune on his presidential run and come away with but a single delegate.

"Riding point leaves you pretty exposed and subject to attack from all sides," Reagan wrote friends on the eve of the 1980 campaign. "Let me tell you . . . I am not changing, have not changed and will not. There wouldn't be any point in seeking that man-killing job if I didn't do it with the idea of working for the principles I believe in. I have discovered out in the country on the trail that if there is any movement, it is the other way—that more Americans than anyone realizes are coming over to our positions."

The chief fear in Reagan circles of support in late 1979 and early 1980 was that somehow Reagan's then campaign chief, John Sears, an old Nixon hand, was domesticating Reagan and pulling him too far to the center. Conservative fears seemed well founded early in the campaign as George H. W. Bush upset Reagan in a well-publicized Iowa straw poll and did so again in the next contest, which was held in Puerto Rico. The Bush surge ended soon enough with a now-legendary debate showdown held in a Nashua, New Hampshire, gym, as Reagan outmaneuvered Bush to win the state. He would sweep through South Carolina and the rest of the South to take a large lead early in the primary season.

As it turned out, any fears of Ronald Reagan being manipulated by a moderate campaign manager were overstated. This was yet another time that conservatives fell into the trap of that fatal liberal flaw: the persistent underestimation of Ronald Reagan.

Reagan proved time and again to be a conservative whose vision of the world was grounded in the principles of individual liberty because he believed liberty was the best way to produce the greatest good for the greatest number. Anything that unreasonably abridged the freedom of man—whether an overreaching government or a totalitarian system—was to be fought. But Reagan also had an uncanny knack for knowing how far voters could be pushed to the right and when it was time to make tough choices. As he declared in his 1976 convention speech, quoting Douglas MacArthur, there was no substitute for victory. Entering a battle to do no more than send a message was out of the question. And if that meant he had to make difficult decisions—like firing his campaign manager on the day of the New Hampshire primary—Reagan did just that.

Ronald Reagan changed the world and revolutionized modern politics not only because of his conservatism but because he possessed the skills necessary to bring his philosophical principles to bear on reality, and reshape that reality. His 1976 foe, President Ford, was a good man but lacked—as most politicians do—the ability to change history in the way Reagan could.

The direction in which Reagan bent the world was determined by the ideas that had been changing the Republican Party for nearly a generation. It was Reagan who combined the intellectual insights of Buckley, the fervor of the Cow Palace, and the cold calculation of Eisenhower to put together an unstoppable campaign in 1980.

What Reagan's opponents—including his Republican rivals for the nomination—failed to recognize as the 1970s drew to a close was that the GOP was no longer really up for grabs and that Reagan was largely correct when he said that the party, with its essential conservatism, was now more reflective of the country than the views of moderate Republicans or FDR Democrats. It was an astounding historic turnaround from the Roosevelt and Truman years.

Two scenes tell the tale. In August, just after the Detroit convention, Reagan went to the Neshoba County Fair in Mississippi. The scene of much tragedy during the civil rights years, Neshoba was, for Reagan, now an emblem of a larger regional and national story: the shift of white Democrats to the Republicans, a process that had begun sixteen years before in the Goldwater campaign.

"I know that in speaking to this crowd, that I'm speaking to what has to be about 90 percent Democrat," Reagan said at the fair. The crowd shouted "No," and Reagan added: "I just meant by party affiliation. I didn't mean how you feel now. I was a Democrat most of my life myself, but then decided that there were things that needed to be changed."

The second scene, at Liberty State Park on Labor Day 1980. Reagan is coatless, his hair and shirt windswept. The Statue of Liberty stands in the background, and the nominee of the party of Dewey and Taft strikes populist notes, arguing that the economic fates of all Americans—rich and poor, satisfied and striving—would be best cared for in his hands, thus reversing decades of political assumption.

Americans were in fact suffering from malaise, and Reagan spelled out why in the starkest of terms.

Eight million out of work. Inflation running at 18 percent in the first quarter of 1980. Black unemployment at about 14 percent, higher than any single year since the government began keeping separate statistics. Four straight major deficits run up by Carter and his friends in Congress. The highest interest rates since the

Civil War—reaching at times close to 20 percent—lately down
to more than 11 percent but now going up again—productivity
falling for six straight quarters among the most productive peo-
ple in history.

Reagan then spoke to the heart of his economic policy—that
lower taxes create jobs and higher taxes destroy the economy.

Through his inflation he has raised taxes on the American
people by 30 percent—while their real income has risen only 20
percent. He promised he would not increase taxes for the low
and middle-income people—the workers of America. Then he
imposed on American families the largest single tax increase in
history.

Reagan showed politicians how to deliver a body blow to a political opponent while keeping a smile on your face and a punch line in
your pocket.

His answer to all of this misery? He tries to tell us that we are
"only" in a recession, not a depression, as if definitions—words—
relieve our suffering. Let it show on the record that when the
American people cried out for economic help, Jimmy Carter
took refuge behind a dictionary. Well, if it's a definition he
wants, I'll give him one. A recession is when your neighbor loses
his job. A depression is when you lose yours. Recovery is when
Jimmy Carter loses his. . . . Call this human tragedy whatever
you want. Whatever it is, it is Jimmy Carter's. He caused it. He

tolerates it. And he is going to answer to the American people for it.

Reagan's speech in front of Lady Liberty looked as if it were produced for an old Warner Bros. classic. The old political actor looked every bit the Hollywood star placed in front of Lady Liberty, and Reagan's strong presence was a striking contrast to Jimmy Carter, especially when considering the run of bad PR the president had suffered over the last year. Carter had collapsed dramatically while jogging in front of the cameras the previous fall and two months earlier even had to endure the *Washington Post* headline "Rabbit Attacks President."

But it wasn't the president's jogging woes or the bizarre story of a killer rabbit attack that was causing President Carter his biggest headaches. That reputation for weakness came from America's economic collapse, the Soviet invasion of Afghanistan, and most damning, the ongoing Iranian hostage crisis that made the United States look impotent in the eyes of the world.

On the campaign trail, Jimmy Carter was fighting yesterday's political battle. His caricature of Reagan was just that—a caricature that history has proven incorrect but one that Carter still believed long after leaving the White House. While there was to be constant conversation through the Reagan years about his actual level of interest in the less fortunate, voters proved to be less skeptical than the press and the political class. Even Richard Wirthlin, Reagan's pollster, worried about Reagan's "negative image [as] an unsympathetic candidate lacking a personal concern for the people's problems of welfare, aging, health care, etc." Yet Reagan won in 1980 and again, thunderously, in 1984—leaving a Republican brand in good enough shape to enable his own vice president to win a successive term, something that had not happened since Martin Van Buren followed Andrew Jackson into the White House in 1837. So the much-talked-about "politics of greed" and critiques of "Reaganomics" were just that: much-talked-about rhetoric that moved few swing voters against Reagan in his two presidential landslide victories and his two landslide wins earlier running for governor of California.

Reagan rose to power as a Main Street conservative with more in common with Eisenhower and Nixon than people generally recognized. Between those three GOP presidents, the party of Lincoln celebrated five landslide victories of the six they ran. Most in the Eastern establishment never saw Ronald Reagan's revolution coming. Particularly President Carter.

Speaking of Reagan and the Republicans in his own acceptance speech at the Democratic National Convention in New York in 1980, Carter said: "In their fantasy America, inner-city people and farm workers and laborers do not exist. Women, like children, are to be seen but not heard. The problems of working women are simply ignored. The elderly do not need Medicare. The young do not need more help in getting a better education. Workers do not require the guarantee of a healthy and a safe place to work. In their fantasy world, all the complex global changes of the world since World War II have never happened. In their fantasy America, all problems have simple solutions—simple and wrong. It's a make-believe world, a world of good guys and bad guys, where some politicians shoot first and ask questions later. No hard choices, no sacrifice, no tough decisions—it sounds too good to be true, and it is."

Later in the fall Carter said outright that the decision in the election would determine "whether we have peace or war," borrowing the Ford sentiment from 1976 that President Reagan would lead America into war. And in a classic moment of political hyperbole, the president of the United States told a fund-raising event: "You'll determine whether or not this America will be unified or, if I lose this election, whether Americans might be separated, black from white, Jew from Christian, North from South, rural from urban."

How simple things would have been for Carter had this two-dimensional portrait of Reagan in fact been grounded in reality.

But it wasn't. Carter darkly warned Americans of Reagan, adopting a clichéd liberal version of the Republican worldview. The president, like all others who ran elections against Reagan, would pay in November for his inability to see Reagan in full.

That complete version of Reagan was on display in the single presidential debate of the fall campaign, in Cleveland, on October 28, just a week out from the balloting. Most commentators considered the debate close until Reagan began his closing argument to the American people. The conservative Californian captured the complexities of the moment brilliantly:

Are you better off now than you were four years ago? Is it easier for you to go and buy things in the stores than it was four years ago? Is there more or less unemployment in the country than there was four years ago? Is America as respected throughout the world as it was? Do you feel that our security is as safe, that we're as strong as we were four years ago? And if you answer all of those questions "yes," why then, I think your choice is very obvious as to whom you will vote for. If you don't agree, if you don't think that this course that we've been on for the last four

years is what you would like to see us follow for the next four,
then I could suggest another choice that you have.

That was the choice Americans made seven days later, giving Reagan an Electoral College landslide and ushering in a new era, albeit one linked to the Eisenhower and Nixon majorities that had preceded it. Reagan was a conservative, but a commonsense conservative who shaped the world in his political image whenever allowed by the political realities of his day. Because of that pragmatic conservatism, every president after him has had to live in the world that Reagan made.

9

You Ain't Seen Nothing Yet

"As an individual you incarnate American ideals at many levels. As the final responsible authority, in any hour of great challenge, we depend on you."
—*William F. Buckley, Jr., to President Reagan, 1985*

"Let us be sure that those who come after will say of us in our time, that in our time we did everything that could be done. We finished the race; we kept them free; we kept the faith."
—*Ronald Reagan, 1984 State of the Union address*

YOU COULD NOT THEN—OR NOW—BUY THE KIND OF COV-erage *Time* magazine gave Ronald Reagan in midsummer 1986. The cover featured a portrait of Reagan with the question, "Why Is This Man So Popular?" Inside, beneath the headline "Yankee Doodle Magic," Lance Morrow wrote:

Ronald Reagan has found the American sweet spot. The white ball sails into the sparkling air in a high parabola and vanishes over the fence, again. The 75-year-old man is hitting home runs. Winning a lopsided vote on a tax-reform plan that others had

airily dismissed. Turning Congress around on the contras. Pre-
paring to stand with a revitalized Miss Liberty on the Fourth of
July. He grins his boyish grin and bobs his head in the way he
has and trots around the bases.

Reagan inhabits his moment in America with a triumphant
(some might say careless or even callous) ease that is astonishing
and even mysterious. . . . He is a Prospero of American memo-
ries, a magician who carries a bright, ideal America like a holo-
graph in his mind and projects its image in the air. . . . Reagan,
master illusionist, is himself a kind of American dream. Look-
ing at his genial, crinkly face prompts a sense of wonder: How
does he pull it off?

His barber, Milton Pitts, reports that when Ronald Reagan
took office his hair was about 25% gray. It is now 30% gray. The
President has added a second hearing aid in the past year or so.
He uses three combinations for his eyes: hard contact lenses for
normal activities, half glasses over the contacts for reading, and
a single contact lens (left eye) for giving speeches on podiums
where he needs to focus on the audience and the TelePrompTer
at the same time. Reagan still has his suits made with buttons
on the flies. He refuses to wear makeup for television. He pumps
iron every day. He rides a horse when he can. His favorite story
is his old surreal barnyard parable regarding optimism—about
the boy who finds a pile of horse manure in a room and cries
excitedly, "I just know there's a pony in here somewhere."

The septuagenarian in the White House is not necessarily
getting any younger. On the other hand, he does not seem to be
getting any older. His suit size has been the same for years—
42—and so have the ideological furnishings of his mind. His

principles give him a certain serenity, and possibly the luck
that comes to the optimist. Reagan keeps finding the pony. He
proceeds, amiably and formidably, from success to success. His
life is a sort of fairy tale of American power. The business of
magic is sleight of hand: now you see it, now you don't. Ronald
Reagan is a sort of masterpiece of American magic—apparently
one of the simplest, most uncomplicated creatures alive, and yet
a character of rich meanings, of complexities that connect him
with the myths and powers of his country in an unprecedented
way.

Time reported another critical fact about Reagan's America: in a
startling reversal from the 1960s, young people identified more with
the aging Republican president than with the Democrats. "A White
House survey for May," the magazine said, "showed that 82% of registered voters age 24 and under approved of Reagan. Says Presidential Pollster Richard Wirthlin: 'This is an age cohort that has known
only two Presidents.' The binary vision of the young: in their memo-
ries, Carter meant failure, Reagan means success."

How did Reagan do it? It wasn't all Prospero and fairy dust. The
Reagan years were substantive ones in constructive conservatism.
He never let the perfect be the enemy of the good, either at home or
abroad, and his presidency will long be a rich source of instruction
and inspiration for conservatives who hope, as Reagan used to say,
to make it the way they want it to be.

Three examples should make the point.

- **Taxes and government.** He arrived in Washington in January 1981 determined to reduce the size and scope of govern-

ment. In the end he couldn't do all—or even as much as—he would have liked. But Ronald Reagan did what was possible.

By passing the Kemp-Roth tax-rate reduction bill in 1981, Reagan reduced marginal income tax rates dramatically. And by successfully pursuing tax reform in 1986, Reagan further reduced the tax burden on most Americans. His relentless focus on the amount of money the federal government took from each taxpayer has dominated the political dynamic in the country ever since. As George H. W. Bush learned when he went along with new tax increases in 1990, breaking his "read my lips" pledge, Americans after Reagan remain deeply skeptical of any plan that takes money out of their pockets and sends it to Washington.

Bill Clinton raised rates, but paid for it in the 1994 Republican landslide. His Democratic successor, Barack Obama, would end up repudiating whatever might have been left of Democratic orthodoxy when he extended George W. Bush's tax cuts through the 2012 election—a sign that Reagan's worldview was now as permanent a part of the American landscape as FDR's had been.

Bill Clinton and Barack Obama were to Ronald Reagan what Dwight Eisenhower and Richard Nixon were to Franklin Roosevelt: ratifiers of the order created by a dominant and enduring president whose long shadow casts itself over Washington policies for generations to come. Even today, most voters have come to expect a government that provides FDR's programs with Reagan's tax rates. One day that ideological conflict will have to be resolved, but few hazard to guess when that will be.

- **The Cold War.** No charge worried Reagan's opponents more, both before and early in his presidency, than the one that cast him as a nuclear cowboy and warmonger. Carter was explicit about this in 1980.

But what happened? The conservative hawk outraged liberal critics by calling nuclear weapon systems "peacemakers," by refusing to back down on his missile defense system, and by disavowing the détente approach favored by Nixon, Ford, and Carter. And while negotiating from a position of strength, Reagan forced the Soviets to enter into deals that helped reduce nuclear arsenals and would eventually lead the United States to victory in the Cold War. He did it by using negotiating skills learned while serving as a liberal Hollywood union leader, starting with a tough bargaining position but gradually finding a way to let his adversary out of the corner.

Of course no single person won the Cold War. What President Kennedy called the "long twilight struggle" required the blood and patience of martyrs behind the Iron Curtain, the bravery of shipyard workers in Gdansk, the quiet witness of the voiceless within the Communist bloc, and the investments of time and treasure made by American presidents of both parties.

But Ronald Reagan did more than any other president to bring a successful end to a conflict that once seemed interminable. The man who had made "détente" a dirty word in Republican politics in the 1970s accomplished more than all the Wise Men and all the *realpolitik* New Yorkers ever had. And he did it, presidential historian Michael Beschloss said, by making a one-trillion-dollar bet that the Soviet leaders could not keep up with spending levels pushed by an American president who was willing to go all in with such a strategic bet. Reagan was right. The USSR was soon reduced to the ash heap of history.

- **Guns.** A longtime Second Amendment guy, Reagan showed pragmatism even on the explosive issue of guns. "With the right to bear arms comes a great responsibility to use caution and common sense on handgun purchases," Reagan said on the tenth anniversary of the assassination attempt on his life. "And it's just plain common sense that there be a waiting period to allow local law-enforcement officials to conduct background checks on those who wish to purchase handguns."

According to *The New York Times,* a National Rifle Association official, on hearing of Reagan's support for the waiting period, gazed at a photo of Reagan on his desk and said, "Don't do this to me."

Then, three years later, Ronald Reagan signed a letter supporting a proposed ban on assault weapons. "This is a matter of vital importance to the public safety," Reagan wrote. "Although assault weapons account for less than 1% of the guns in circulation, they account for nearly 10% of the guns traced to crime. . . . While we recognize that assault-weapon legislation will not stop all assault-weapon crime, statistics prove that we can dry up the supply of these guns, making them less accessible to criminals. We urge you to listen to the American public and to the law enforcement community and support a ban on the further manufacture of these weapons."

Reagan famously was responsible for the bill's passage by

picking up the phone and calling wavering GOP congress-
men. His final call to Wisconsin Republican Scott Klug gave
the congressman the courage needed to cast the deciding vote
for the legislation. Even out of office, Ronald Reagan's pragmatic conservatism held sway over swing voters.

In 1985, at the thirtieth anniversary dinner for *National Review* at
the Plaza Hotel in New York, Bill Buckley directly addressed his fellow guest, President Ronald Reagan.

"As an individual you incarnate American ideals at many levels,"
Buckley said to the president. "As the final responsible authority, in
any hour of great challenge, we depend on you." Buckley was nineteen when America dropped the bomb at Hiroshima, he said, and he
had just turned sixty. "During the interval I have lived a free man in
a free and sovereign country, and this only because we have hus-
banded a nuclear deterrent, and made clear our disposition to use it
if necessary. I pray that my son, when he is 60, and your son, when
he is 60 . . . will live in a world from which the great ugliness that has
scarred our century has passed. Enjoying their freedoms, they will
be grateful that, at the threatened nightfall, the blood of their fathers
ran strong."

Four years later, Ronald Reagan would board Marine One to leave
the Capitol grounds in the moments after the inauguration of
George Herbert Walker Bush for his first journey back to California
as a former president. Because Reagan's blood did run strong, and
because he was so wonderfully equipped to ignore the chorus of critics who questioned his judgment and smarts on a daily basis, he
could fly westward into the setting sun with the assurance that in his

time he had done everything that could be done. "We finished the race; we kept them free; we kept the faith."

Within months of Reagan's retirement, the Warsaw Pact's foundation began cracking apart. Soon after, the Berlin Wall fell, the Soviet empire collapsed in ruins, and 100 million souls across Europe were set free. Millions of those liberated souls would rightly credit Ronald Reagan for their newfound freedom.

10

The Polo Populist

"I do not hate government. A government that remembers
that the people are its master is a good and needed thing."
—*George H. W. Bush, accepting the*
1988 *Republican presidential nomination*

IT WAS, IT BECAME CLEAR LATER, THE MOST MOMENTOUS OF
Halloweens, and the most significant Republican political incident
involving pumpkins since Richard Nixon's investigators marched
across a Maryland field toward a hollowed-out pumpkin to find mi-
crofilm that would lead to Alger Hiss's conviction. In Aiken, South
Carolina, some time later, the Atwaters moved to town. A neighbor,
United States senator Strom Thurmond, was always generous with
Halloween candy. "He came out and gave me a Snickers candy bar,"
recalled Lee Atwater, the future GOP warrior, according to a biography by John Brady. "That was the best thing I got that year. So I liked
Senator Thurmond, but I didn't know anything about politics."

That would change soon enough. Today, Lee Atwater rightly lives
on in historical memory as the legendary Boy Wonder of hardball
politics for Republican operatives. Atwater brought a "kick-ass"
Southern ethos to the buttoned-down world of George Herbert

Walker Bush, catapulting an elite Yankee dynasty into the White House with rough-and-tumble tactics that Bush could never have dreamt of in his previous political campaigns.

After 1988 it would take another sixteen years for an American president to move into the White House with more than 50 percent of the popular vote. The closely divided electorate that followed Bush 41's victory as well as those scorched-earth, win-at-all-costs tactics have made governing more difficult. Bill Clinton, George W. Bush, and Barack Obama all won reelection in the post-Atwater era but all three also spent their presidencies fighting for their political lives in a city where politics has become a blood sport without end.

This is not to suggest that the forty-one presidents who preceded Bill Clinton were treated with fawning respect by their adversaries. Conspiracy theories spread among paranoid extremists suggested that George H. W. Bush ran drugs, that LBJ planned JFK's assassination, and that Kennedy himself was a Communist sympathizer. But these crazy theories never gained traction because their publication was usually limited to local newspaper ads or cheap paperback books.

Starting in the 1990s, the burgeoning information revolution allowed libelous claims to be sent first by fax, then by email, then website, then instantaneous tweet. Within a short period of time, email replaced mail, Internet servers replaced printing presses, and outrageous political accusations replaced printed stories that were fact-checked before being published by organizations that could lose reputation and money if they got a story wrong.

The toxic culture of new media only accelerated a process in which websites, talk radio hosts, and prime-time cable personalities reduced politics to a blood sport waged by multimillionaire entertainers who became fabulously wealthy by stoking political resentment at both extremes of American life.

The result has been lucrative for those who have mastered the art of the extreme. Books blasting conservatives as "big fat idiots" and trashing liberals as traitors have sold millions. Talk radio hosts who shamelessly stole from Rush Limbaugh's playbook in hopes of making his $40 million a year saw their ratings steadily rise while primetime cable news hosts went from calling Bill Clinton a traitor, to calling George W. Bush a Nazi, to calling Barack Obama a racist who hates all white people. In this vulgarized media landscape, hate is a hot commodity, and many of those peddling it have made themselves very rich. But this new, bitter political climate has been very bad politically for any Republicans who actually want their party running the White House again.

In the two decades since conservative talk radio exploded onto the scene with the national launch of *The Rush Limbaugh Show,* Republican presidential candidates have lost the popular vote in five of six presidential elections. The political value of an army of shrill Limbaugh clones is suspect at best. The 2012 election illustrated just how dangerous it can be for conservative candidates and strategists to encase themselves inside the conservative media bubble, where they are at risk of repeating the mistakes of Mitt Romney—who still believed he would defeat Barack Obama well into the election night.

I am a consumer of conservative news through websites, talk radio, and Fox News. But I also balance news sources that play to my ideological preferences with those that do not. Unfortunately, many conservative thought leaders now limit their media choices to the most extreme voices inside a perpetual right-wing resentment machine. This means the GOP is far more likely to be blindsided, like most conservative leaders in 2012.

The mere suggestion that Mitt Romney's campaign was inept and outdated drew angry responses from the Conservative Entertainment Complex and an immediate accusation that anyone suggesting Barack Obama was on his way to reelection was not a real Republican. The fact was that many who offered warnings to Romney were committed Republicans. They also happened to be committed to the truth.

After Barack Obama's convincing reelection victory, Newt Gingrich admitted that Republicans had damaged their chances by remaining in a conservative echo chamber that never allowed unpleasant political realities to be taken seriously: "I think conservatives in general got in the habit of talking to themselves. I think that they in a sense got isolated into their own little world. So did our pollsters, many of whom were wrong about turnout." The former speaker concluded that Republicans were "just kidding ourselves."

The isolated nature of right-wing alternative media was met during the Bush years by extreme voices on the left, who would even declare nightly who the "worst person in the world" was. A multitude of cable shows and websites on the far left followed suit, spending eight years comparing George W. Bush, Dick Cheney, Verizon, and a multitude of other persons, places, or things to Adolf Hitler's Nazi regime (which, of course, slaughtered six million Jews). Subtlety hasn't been the order of the day for the past few decades, and that's fine with these carnival barkers, because in this new media landscape, subtlety rarely sells.

But in 1988, George H. W. Bush was a man born and bred for the politics of a different era. His father, Prescott Bush, served a decade representing Connecticut in the United States Senate, winning a reputation for steadiness of character and clearheaded moderation. Senator Bush dared to take on Joe McCarthy in 1952, the year Eisenhower himself failed to confront the Wisconsin senator's outrageous claim that one of America's great generals was a Communist. Bush also led federal urban renewal efforts and cosponsored the legislation that created the Peace Corps. Senator Bush left an enduring stamp on his son George, who revered his father and twice tried—and twice failed—to follow Prescott Bush to the Senate.

Senator Bush was an Eisenhower Republican at a time when the base of the party believed that Prescott Bush was far too liberal. His son, Vice President Bush, spent eight years by Ronald Reagan's side, shaking his head in wonder at his boss's ability to communicate a conservative message with such conviction and effectiveness while governing from a political position not so far from his moderate father's.

The Bush answer to the dilemma of how to break the Martin Van Buren curse (in 1836 Van Buren had been the last sitting vice president to win the presidency) was found in Atwaterism: appeal to fundamental virtues of patriotism while painting your opponent as a hapless McGovern liberal.

While more cynical than civil, the Atwater strategy may have been Bush's only path forward in the late summer of 1988 after he had fallen twenty points behind Massachusetts governor Michael Dukakis. The choice had to be excruciating for Prescott Bush's son. George H. W. Bush's attitudes were formed in a different political time. Yet he found himself on the fault line of American politics and had to know by the summer of 1988 that he could not defeat a national Democratic machine obsessed with regaining the White House after eight years of Reaganomics as a refined Connecticut gentleman.

Whereas Ronald Reagan could play against type by moving to the political middle to win swing voters, Bush had to move hard right to lock down a base that had never trusted him. Conservatives didn't seem to like Bush any more than the national press corps did. So the vice president hired Atwater and future Fox News chief Roger Ailes to work miracles in his uphill battle. He also moved his Texas-raised son George W. to Washington to keep an eye on the political team. By the fall of 1988, the vice president was boating across Boston Harbor and touring flag factories to underscore his support for the Pledge of Allegiance. Governor Dukakis had vetoed a bill mandating that the pledge be said in the classrooms of the Commonwealth of Massachusetts.

At heart Bush was a pragmatist in the Eisenhower-Reagan tradition, and he believed—correctly—that Dukakis was too liberal for the American mainstream. To say that Bush won the 1988 race through right-wing pandering is just wrong—the sitting vice president was convincingly elected president by a public that knew him for his formidable résumé and his connection with Reagan, and knew Dukakis by the Massachusetts governor's more extreme views.

But four years later, Lee Atwater was dead, the economy was adrift, and George Bush saw an 89 percent approval rating evaporate in a year. The forty-first president lost his reelection bid in 1992 in large part because he had broken with the party's base in the summer of 1990. In budget talks with congressional Democrats held at

Andrews Air Force Base, Bush agreed to revenue increases as part of a deal that established "pay-go" rules, meaning any future spending hike had to be paid for.

Commentators praised the president for having the courage to stake out a position so unpopular with his own party. Bush had put his credibility as a conservative on the line in 1988 when he told Republicans at the convention that would elevate him to the presidency: "Read my lips: no new taxes." The right appropriately felt betrayed.

Now there were new taxes and the political impact was disastrous for the sitting president. The patrician Bush had just confirmed conservatives' worst fears. He had been true to himself—to his pragmatism—even when breaking a promise to the American people. It was a broken promise that would cost him the presidency.

The scope of conservative outrage over the president's compromise on taxes was obscured for a time by the first Gulf War, which consumed American attention from the Iraqi invasion of Kuwait on August 2, 1990, until well into the triumphant spring of 1991. What was out of sight, though, was not out of the conservative mind.

Enter Pat Buchanan. Or, more formally, Patrick Joseph Buchanan, the former *St. Louis Globe-Democrat* editorial writer, Nixon speechwriter, Reagan communications director, and *Crossfire* cohost. For Buchanan and millions of conservatives, the Andrews deal was a classic establishment sellout of genuine American values—a kind of domestic Yalta, harking back to the old charges about FDR that had shaped conservative beliefs nearly half a century before.

Launching an insurgent primary challenge to Bush, Buchanan merrily railed against "King George" and shocked the political world in New Hampshire. The early returns had Buchanan pulling well over 40 percent from the sitting president, and while he ended the night with a 37 percent share, the result still sent a chilling signal to the Bush White House. One close observer, Bill Clinton, who came in second in the Democratic primary to Paul Tsongas, noted Buchanan's showing and the fact that Bush's national approval numbers had dipped below 50 percent for the first time since the Gulf War. "Although [Bush] still led both Paul Tsongas and me in the polls," Clinton wrote later, "the Democratic nomination was clearly worth having."

George W. Bush would long blame Pat Buchanan for his father's loss to Bill Clinton, and he was not alone. Buchanan's insurgent campaign in New Hampshire and his flaming rhetoric at the 1992 Republican National Convention later that summer have had a surprisingly lasting and underappreciated impact on the Republican Party. Months before Ross Perot stole the national spotlight with a populist campaign against free trade and for balanced budgets, Pat Buchanan was assembling a pitchfork brigade prepared to take on the establishment both in Washington and on Wall Street. And after Bush's loss to Clinton, a new crop of conservative populists began planning runs for Congress in the mold of Buchanan. Within two years, the GOP would control the U.S. House for the first time in forty years, thanks to an incoming freshman class far closer ideologically to the socially conservative, fair trade, noninterventionist policies of Buchanan than they were to George H. W. Bush or Bill Clinton.

Buchanan populism may not have been expansive enough to carry a candidate into the Oval Office, but it revolutionized the modern Republican Party by providing the blueprint to a GOP congressional majority. Buchanan's conservative populism was especially persuasive in districts like my own where Republicans rarely won congressional races. It was persuasive because so many of his policy positions were outside a Washington Republican mainstream that all too often capitulated to big business and big government even when it was not the conservative thing to do.

The coming Republican Revolution of 1994 mixed Buchanan populism with mainstream GOP orthodoxy. Newt Gingrich put together a winning political strategy that kept Republicans in the speaker's chair in the U.S. House of Representatives for sixteen of the past twenty years. But the question Republicans need to answer sooner rather than later is whether the same political tactics that help conservatives win big in gerrymandered congressional districts builds a party that plays well in legislative battles but damages Republicans' efforts on the national level. The answer today clearly seems to be "yes."

Going into the 1992 presidential campaign, Republicans still seemed to have the market cornered when it came to White House real estate. Before the 1992 primaries began, smart money was betting that the GOP's twelve-year reign in the White House would be extended through 1996. President Bush was so popular in 1991 that Democratic leaders thought of as serious potential challengers for the presidency simply stayed away.

But not the governor of Arkansas. In 1992 Bill Clinton shifted the debate away from ideology by borrowing from Michael Dukakis's 1988 convention theme that his campaign would be more about competence. Like Dukakis, Clinton knew that his best chance to take the White House back from Republicans would be to avoid openly ideological fights with a GOP president while American politics remained in a conservative epoch that was launched by Reagan's 1966 victory in California.

Clinton avoided open warfare with Republicans on an ideological battlefield by marching away from the Democratic Party's left-wing position of reflexively supporting an exploding welfare state. Clinton, instead, used his acceptance speech at Madison Square Garden to promote a post-ideological "Third Way" approach that moved beyond the Democrats' big-government ambitions for a simple promise to make government work better for all Americans. Since George H. W. Bush had proven himself to be a big-government Republican and seemed no more interested in reducing the size of the federal bureaucracy than any other Washington politicians, Clinton asked why voters shouldn't give a New Democrat from the South a chance?

The Democratic nominee told the conventioneers that Mr. Bush should "give our people the kind of government they deserve, a government that works for them," declaring that "a President ought to be a powerful force for progress. But right now I know how President Lincoln felt when General McClellan wouldn't attack in the Civil War. He asked him, 'If you're not going to use your army, may I borrow it?' "

Clinton then delivered his punch line to a rapturous Garden. "And so I say: George Bush, if you won't use our power to help America, step aside. I will!"

Before that convention address, the Man from Hope had entered his own convention behind Ross Perot and George H. W. Bush in the polls. By the time Clinton and Al Gore left on a bus tour of America, most political observers were convinced that his last-place position would change quickly.

They were right. In the end, it wasn't even close. Bill Clinton and his promise of a New Democratic path forward ended the GOP's quarter-century grip on the West Wing.

In a withering front-page postmortem story the day after the 1992 election, Maureen Dowd of *The New York Times* captured the defeated president's mood in memorable prose. "It was beginning to sink in, very painfully, that he had been fired," Dowd wrote, "and now he was expected to go back to Washington and take all his stuff out of the Oval Office, the worn Yale baseball mitt, the drawers full of tennis balls, the family pictures, the black and white horseshoes, his black Swiss army knife with 'President Bush' engraved in silver."

George Herbert Walker Bush was a man caught between two political worlds that were pulling apart, and in the end, the center could not hold. Bush was an Eisenhower moderate at heart, but the base of his party was moving rightward, away from the principled pragmatism that won national elections. With Clinton in the White House, Republicans would move into this new era with mixed results. A new Republican congressional majority would soon arise, but the party of Ike and Reagan would lose five out of the next six popular votes for president. This new Republican Party would trade the power of the presidency for the speaker's gavel over the next twenty years. That exchange seems about as balanced as the one that gave Dutch traders possession of Manhattan in 1626 for beads worth twenty-four dollars.

The only question now is when Republicans will realize that they have been scammed.

11

A Revolution Unravels

"We will build an American community again. The choice
we offer is not conservative or liberal. In many ways, it is
not even Republican or Democratic. It is different. It is
new. And it will work."
—*Bill Clinton, accepting the*
1992 Democratic presidential nomination

"There is a Democratic Party that rejects the lessons of
American history, despises the values of the American
people, and denies the basic goodness of the American nation."
—*Newt Gingrich, addressing the*
1992 Republican National Convention

THE WORDS ABOVE DO MORE THAN DRAW A BRIGHT LINE
between the political temperaments of Bill Clinton and Newt
Gingrich. They also vividly illustrate the failings of the two men
who would dominate American politics throughout the 1990s. Bill
Clinton's promise of post-partisanship proved to be a sham in the
first years of his presidency. Once Clinton was elected, his administration darted left on social issues, health care reform, and tax hikes.
Democrats would pay a heavy price two years after Clinton's elec-

tion as Republicans seized control of Congress for the first time in forty years.

The Republican who would become speaker would be the same one telling Americans two years earlier that Democrats ignore history, despise American values, and deny the goodness of America. Working on the congressional rather than the presidential level— harsh ideology works better, at least for a time, down-ballot— Gingrich would use scorched-earth tactics to transform the most liberal governing institution in Washington, D.C., into its most conservative. The achievement was breathtaking—and as with most conservative revolts, it caught Washington and New York's ruling class off guard. Remember, though, that Gingrich was seeking control of the House, not the White House. As the last half century has shown, Republicans may become speakers using the voice of absolutism, but they do not become presidents.

A case in point: As Gingrich was storming toward a shocking victory in South Carolina's presidential primary eighteen years later, many admirers drew comparisons between the former House speaker and Winston Churchill, who had made his own political comeback in the early days of World War II. Gingrich's comeback would, of course, end around a week later, amid attack ads aired by Mitt Romney. Americans may give in to off-year anger, but they are much less inclined to entrust ultimate presidential authority to those who seem more ideological than pragmatic.

Still, Gingrich is an important figure in the story of the post–World War II Republican Party. And one comparison with Churchill does hold true: Newton Leroy Gingrich was and remains a man of ideas, ideas that possess a great fluidity. Just as Churchill found himself holding conflicting positions through his long career, Gingrich has philosophically belonged to nearly every tribe or belief system that has informed the Republican Party in the decades since Eisenhower. Gingrich ran for Congress unsuccessfully in 1974 and 1976 as a moderate before winning in 1978 as a conservative. He was a self-described Rockefeller Republican. He was also a self-described Goldwater Republican.

He later embraced Reagan, frequently portraying himself during the 2012 presidential campaign as a soldier of the Reagan Revolution. He also criticized Reagan (with characteristic verbosity), saying things like "The Reagan failure was to grossly undervalue the centrality of government as the organizing mechanism for reinforcing societal behavior."

Gingrich—like his chief political nemesis, Bill Clinton—was a Southern-based baby boomer driven by political ideas. He had spent much of the 1980s cultivating a GOP base of conservatives who agreed with Bill Bennett, James Dobson, and the Heritage Foundation that the United States entered the 1990s facing not merely a political but a civilizational crisis. In late-night C-SPAN speeches to an empty House, in GOPAC audio- and videotapes sent to prospective candidates, and in numerous national interviews not usually afforded to a backbencher in the minority party, Gingrich, a former history professor, astutely discerned and tapped into deep cultural conflicts that, born in the 1960s, still boiled just below the surface of American society.

Though fascinated by the future, Gingrich practiced a politics of nostalgia that borrowed more from the resentments of Richard Nixon than the optimism of Ronald Reagan. He may not have been the campaigner that either of those GOP giants were, but Gingrich was a political visionary whose audacious belief that the Republican

Party could once again control Congress was mocked by almost every respected observer in Washington.

I personally remember entering RNC headquarters in the summer of 1993 and being greeted by a sign that said "Think Majority." Such a thought that year was so preposterous that I let out a reflexive laugh despite the fact I was there to run for Congress hoping to represent a part of Florida that had not sent a Republican to Congress since 1873. No Republican leader I spoke with in 1994 actually believed the GOP could gain control of the House of Representatives unless they were inside the Georgia congressman's inner circle. Gingrich and his team would soon prove the entire political world wrong.

Despite facing doubters throughout his political career, Newt Gingrich was certain of his place in history and always knew he would become the first GOP speaker of the House since Sam Rayburn held the gavel in 1955. According to a *Washington Post* report based on archives from Gingrich's early days in the House, the future speaker had few self-esteem issues. "When I say save the West, I mean that," Gingrich said in 1979. "That is my job. . . . It is not my job to win reelection. It is not my job to take care of passport problems. It is not my job to get a bill through Congress. My job description as I have defined it is to save Western civilization." He also told the *Post* on the eve of Ronald Reagan's second inauguration, "I have enormous personal ambition. I want to shift the entire planet. And I'm doing it. I am now a famous person. I represent real power."

In a book published a decade later when he did in fact possess "real power," Gingrich praised what was good about the country, but then let readers know just how America had been taken off its proper course.

"A sense of anxiety has increased in America," Gingrich wrote in *To Renew America*. "Nor are these anxieties groundless. How can any American watching the local television news not have a sense of alarm? Children being abused or killed, mothers being murdered in car-jackings, innocent customers shot in robberies. Young men are without education, without jobs, without hope for their own or their younger brothers' futures."

Bill Clinton somewhat grudgingly acknowledged Gingrich's purely tactical ability to fire up the GOP base. In his memoirs, Clinton seemed to possess a grudging admiration for Gingrich's attacking the first couple as "counterculture McGovernicks"—which was, Clinton noted later, Gingrich's "ultimate condemnation."

It worked. Bill and Hillary Clinton's mandate of 1992 was quickly swept aside by an electorate who punished the Arkansas "New Democrat" for spending his first two years in the Oval Office governing like an old-time liberal. Many, including myself, believe that if Bill Clinton had shown the courage to cross his left-wing base and push for moderate measures like welfare reform in 1993 and 1994, he would have helped his party hold on to power. Instead, the Clinton administration got bogged down in battles over guns, gays, and a nationalized health care plan that drove away middle-class voters. The Clintons may simply have been ahead of their time, but regardless, the man who many hailed as the greatest Democratic politician since JFK misread the electorate terribly his first two years in office.

Election results in 1994 showed that Americans agreed with Gingrich, not Clinton, and believed that something had gone terribly wrong in America. For those who sought change, the new speaker did not disappoint. The U.S. House passed sweeping congressional reforms the day the new majority was sworn into Congress and immediately started hammering away at big deficits, high taxes, and a bloated welfare state. During his time as speaker, the United States balanced the budget for the first time in a generation, balanced it four years in a row for the first time since the 1920s, made actual cuts in federal spending, passed welfare reform, cut capital gains taxes, cut the inheritance tax, passed sweeping regulatory reform, and did most of this only after dragging a reluctant Bill Clinton to the table.

If political power is defined by reshaping the debate to the contours of your beliefs, Newt Gingrich possessed tremendous power throughout the 1990s. Most telling was Bill Clinton's admission (in his autobiography) that his two most important accomplishments as president were a balanced budget and welfare reform. Considering that President Clinton allowed the federal government to shut down rather than agree to a seven-year balanced budget deal, and then vetoed two welfare reform bills that resembled the third version that he signed, it's clear that no single political figure defined the Clinton presidency at home more than Newt Gingrich.

Gingrich's impact on policy was considered overwhelmingly positive for conservative Republicans. He was the man who more than anyone else brought the Reagan Revolution to the legislative branch. But he did so while employing the Atwater strategy to win elections. While the approach was usually successful at the polls, Republican candidates often found themselves backing away from Gingrichian statements such as the one suggesting that Democratic ideas were responsible for a mother drowning her children. Many Republicans also became disillusioned with his management of the House. At one closed-door meeting of the GOP caucus, Ways and Means chairman Bill Thomas joined the chorus of freshman members attacking the speaker by saying, "Newt, you can tell us where civilization will be in 50 years. You just aren't capable of knowing what we are going to be doing on the House floor next week." All this while Gingrich continued telling advisers and close friends that his mission was to save Western Civilization from collapse.

Newt Gingrich's political grandiosity was to prove fatal. "I am the right wing," he told *Newsweek* in 1996 even as he was beginning to fend off the attacks from fellow conservatives that would eventually be his undoing. Those closest to him often complained that Gingrich was a kind of historical Walter Mitty, forever analogizing the struggles of the 1990s to the Napoleonic Wars or the American Civil War or to whatever other sweeping event that happened to cross his mind. But Newt's fall was still in the future—as was his rise, for that matter—on the January morning in 1993 when Bill Clinton delivered an inaugural address that he had written in a characteristically chaotic fashion. "There is nothing wrong with America that cannot be cured by what is right with America," said Clinton. "And so today we pledge an end to the era of deadlock and drift, and a new season of American renewal has begun."

Or not, as it turned out.

Clinton's promise of post-partisanship got off to a messy start, with battles over nominees, gay marriage, and abortion. His promise of a middle-class tax cut—the pledge that had seemed to salvage his scandal-ridden New Hampshire campaign—was quickly tossed aside in favor of a massive tax increase and a health care plan organized and run by his wife. The Clintons' first two years were the most explosive in Washington since Hillary Rodham worked on the House Judiciary Committee as a staffer focused on the impeachment of Richard Nixon. While the young Democratic president was successful pushing through a tax increase, NAFTA, a crime bill, and other significant legislation, the consensus of most disinterested observers was that Clinton was pulled left by a Democratic Congress that had little interest in softening their liberal agenda after a decade of Reaganism. From Florida, I watched Bill Clinton drag senior Democratic leaders to the left on taxes, guns, and spending bills. Within months of his inauguration, I knew I had a chance to defeat a sixteen-year Democratic incumbent despite the fact that I was a twenty-nine-year-old rookie with little money, no name ID, and no connections in politics. When I began campaigning full-time later in the year, it became evident that I would not be running against the Democratic incumbent; I would be running a campaign against Bill Clinton.

The left wing of the president's party controlled the agenda during Clinton's first two years in office but it came at a calamitous cost to the Democratic House, which lost its majority for the first time in forty years. The speaker of the House, Tom Foley, lost his seat in Washington State, while other Democratic heavyweights were swept aside by a Republican revolution that sent seventy-four GOP freshmen to Washington at the start of the 104th Congress. Gingrich and his Contract with America soon became the dominant forces in Washington, D.C., while the president of the United States, who just two years earlier promised to transform the country, lost control of the agenda in a manner almost historic for a president.

Republicans stormed Capitol Hill and passed a flurry of nonideological reforms on their first day in power. The speed and effectiveness of their efforts dramatically shifted power to the GOP House as Newt Gingrich became the most powerful force in Washington politics. He had united the Republican Party despite the resentment of some older GOP bulls. *Time* named him Person of the Year, and specific legislation in his Contract with America was embraced by most Americans and a large number of Democrats voting in the House. Many of the reforms seemed obvious and bipartisan:

1. Require all laws that apply to the rest of the country also apply to Congress;
2. Select a major, independent auditing firm to conduct a comprehensive audit of Congress for waste, fraud, or abuse;
3. Cut the number of House committees, and cut committee staff by one-third;
4. Limit the terms of all committee chairs;
5. Ban the casting of proxy votes in committee;
6. Require committee meetings to be open to the public;
7. Require a three-fifths majority vote to pass a tax increase;
8. Guarantee an honest accounting of the federal budget by implementing zero baseline budgeting

After Gingrich delivered a nationally televised address following the first hundred days of the new GOP Congress, Clinton found himself explaining to members of the White House press corps that he was still relevant to events in Washington if for no other reason than the U.S. Constitution said so.

Within a week, Clinton would find his voice: in the aftermath of the Oklahoma City bombing of the Alfred P. Murrah Federal Building in 1995, he turned that tragic event against his adversaries on talk radio by indirectly blaming them for the deaths of 168 Americans in a speech. He would attack talk radio even more directly during a background discussion with the White House press corps aboard Air Force One.

"The atmosphere of hostility [against government] was intensified by right-wing radio talk-show hosts, whose venomous rhetoric pervaded the airwaves daily," Clinton wrote after his presidency, "and by Web sites encouraging people to rise up against the government and offering practical assistance, including easy-to-follow instructions on how to make bombs."

Much like the shooting of Congresswoman Gabby Giffords in 2011, the wave of horror following Timothy McVeigh's terrorist acts marked a turning point in the life of the nation in the 1990s, beginning with what Clinton called "a slow but inexorable moving away from the kind of uncritical condemnation that had become all too prevalent in our political life."

Back in Washington, meanwhile, the quick victories of Gingrich's first hundred days would be bogged down by proposed Medicare cuts, a government shutdown, and ethics charges against the new Republican speaker.

Clinton had fought back from political defeat before, following his 1980 gubernatorial loss in Arkansas, and was using a Republican operative, Dick Morris, to slow the GOP's legislative momentum. (Clinton gave Morris the code name "Charlie" to hide the pollster's role from the White House staff.) Already burned by the Democrats' most progressive wing on the Hill, Clinton spent 1995 and 1996 triangulating against their liberal excesses and painting the Gingrich Congress as heartless radicals.

The Morris strategy worked wonders for the Clinton White House. The same president who was routed in his first midterm election as an out-of-touch liberal admitted to the first Republican Congress in more than a generation that, on health care, "We bit off more than we could chew." The next year Clinton went further, declaring "the era of big government is over." That was not, however, the whole sentence. Anticipating the rise of Barack Obama a decade later—a rise that included defeating Hillary Clinton in the 2008 primary season—Clinton went on: "But we cannot go back to the time when our citizens were left to fend for themselves. We must go forward as one America, one nation working together, to meet the challenges we face together. Self-reliance and teamwork are not opposing virtues—we must have both." Clinton's triangulation had the effect of strangulation on the Republican Revolution of 1994.

The president alternately charmed and outfoxed the speaker. ("I melt when I'm around him," Gingrich said of Clinton, to the horror of my congressional classmates.) After a joint town hall meeting in New Hampshire in 1995 in which Clinton and Gingrich shook hands on a deal to work for campaign finance reform, Rush Limbaugh and New Hampshire's conservative *Manchester Union-Leader* attacked Newt, as Clinton put it, for being "too pleasant to me." But the fact was that for all of his verbal attacks on the Clintons, the man who brought the Reagan Revolution to Capitol Hill could have used the Gipper's remarkable negotiating skills while taking on Clinton. Gingrich, the long-term visionary, proved incapable of short-term strategic thinking in his first two years as speaker. He would admit to a stunned GOP caucus that the president always got the better of him in budget negotiations.

"I've never seen anything like it," the speaker told his anxious troops during the 1995 shutdown. "You give this guy everything you have in your wallet and then he makes you feel bad for not having more to give him!" That strange dynamic that made Gingrich "melt" at his very presence also made the Georgian back down at critical times during the government shutdown, despite the fact that Clinton's numbers had begun to fall just before Speaker Gingrich panicked and reopened the government on the president's terms. Gingrich went to Republican members in the Cannon Caucus Room, begging them to vote to reopen the government and saying that if he were going to continue as speaker, the conference would have to give him this vote.

It seems strange looking back that after the midterm disaster of 1994, Bill Clinton tacked to the center and seemed to understand the Eisenhower-Reagan tradition of pragmatism better than those of us in the Gingrich Congress. The same politicians who took control of Congress to act as a check on Clinton radicalism helped reelect the forty-second president by looking radical themselves to many voters. Many in 1996 were less interested in saving Western Civilization or refighting the cultural battles of the 1960s than they were in keeping the government open and the strong economy going. Reflecting on the Gingrich Congress and its obsession with the 1960s, Clinton took a different view.

"Of course there were political and personal excesses in the 1960s, but the decade and the movements it spawned also produced advances in civil rights, women's rights, a clean environment, workplace safety, and opportunities for the poor," Clinton wrote later. "The Democrats believed in and worked for those things. So did a lot of traditional Republicans, including many of the governors I'd served with in the late 1970s and 1980s."

Bill Clinton got reelected in 1996 as a centrist by talking about balancing the budget and passing welfare reform instead of the great strides made by the left in the 1960s. That centrist tone was the political voice the country wanted—just as in the presidential elections that gave Ike, Nixon, and Reagan massive landslide victories. Oklahoma City, Mediscare, and the government shutdown combined to make Clinton once again seem like the safe, moderate choice, rather than the conservative Republicans—myself included—who preferred to keep trying to push the country further right than reality permitted. The same voters who gave the White House to Clinton in 1992 and Congress to Gingrich in 1994 abruptly shifted their allegiances back to the Democratic standard-bearer in 1996. And just as Democrats paid for their partisan excesses in 1994, Republicans would pay an equally heavy price for their excesses in Clinton's re-election campaign in 1996.

It was hard for me to grasp then, but the same Republicans who elected conservatives like Joe Scarborough, Steve Largent, and Tom Coburn to Congress in 1994 chose as presidential nominee Kansas moderate Bob Dole in 1996. It was as if our own base realized that the GOP had taken the party too far right in two years and it was time to answer that action with a more moderate reaction. It was Bob Dole's turn, but the wry Capitol Hill deal maker did not translate very well outside Kansas or the Nebraska Avenue NW studios of NBC's *Meet the Press*. Wounded in war, trained in the art of compromise and pragmatism in Washington, Dole represented an older, different kind of politics. In many ways he was well suited to be a good president, who knew how to make Washington work and distrusted reflexive ideology. But faced with Bill Clinton, the contest was never really close.

Four years into the post–Cold War political era, then, power between the parties had effectively shifted three times. (Democrats won in 1992; Republicans in 1994; Democrats in 1996.) Talk of impeachment in 1998 over the president's Monica Lewinsky affair actually added to Democratic gains in that year's midterm elections, leading to Gingrich's stunning resignation as speaker only four years after the great victory of 1994.

Newt Gingrich had lost the confidence of the very conservatives that he helped elect just a few years earlier. Ever the political tactician, Speaker Gingrich concluded early on that he could move from the speaker's chair to the Oval Office only by moving away from the divisive tactics that were necessary to start the kind of political earthquake that would shake loose the Democratic Party's iron grip on Congress. But the method by which he achieved that unlikely goal made his downfall a Democratic obsession even before he was sworn in as speaker. Democratic House whip David Bonior led his party's efforts in leveling a flurry of ethics charges against the new speaker in the hope that one of them would stick. Gingrich, for his part, moved quickly in his new speakership to reach out to the same political enemies he was blasting as McGovernicks just a few months earlier.

In a swearing-in ceremony that played more like a miniature presidential inauguration, Gingrich tried quickly to make the transition from back-bench bomb thrower to post-partisan political leader. His first speech as speaker sought common ground with Democrats, noting his friendship with minority leader Dick Gephardt, the "extraordinary generosity" of departing speaker Tom Foley, and the historic contributions of FDR. The same politician who, days before the 1994 election, seemingly imputed blame to Democrats for a mother's drowning of her two children was now offering an extended hand to Democrats.

I want us to dedicate ourselves to reach out in a genuinely non-partisan way to be honest with each other. I promise each of you that without regard to party my door is going to be open. I will listen to each of you. I will try to work with each of you. I will put in long hours, and I will guarantee that I will listen to you first.

. . . I want to close by reminding all of us of how much bigger this is than us.

Despite the uplifting oratory, neither the Democratic Party nor the liberal press shared the new speaker's interest in letting bygones be bygones. Following his elevation to the speakership, Gingrich faced unprecedented scrutiny and hostility. As long as the slings and arrows were sailing in from the direction of Massachusetts congressman Barney Frank and the editorial pages of *The New York Times,* the Georgia conservative could survive. But his continued efforts to gain some level of acceptance from Bill Clinton and liberal elites who would never accept him as worthy of being in their social stratum may have led Gingrich to accommodate President Clinton in budget talks more often than not, and to distance himself from the GOP freshmen whose victories were owed, in part, to the speaker.

Even before the 1998 election, Gingrich had struck out on the House floor and attacked conservatives like myself for being members of the "perfectionist caucus." His frustration with our group of hard-liners boiled over in private meetings, caucus events, and now on the House floor. The end was near.

A day after the disappointing midterm elections, Arizona congressman Matt Salmon called to tell me he had the votes to remove Gingrich as speaker. He asked that I call the speaker's most trusted political adviser, Joe Gaylord, since it was Joe whose campaign management school had helped me run an underfunded campaign to victory. After telling Gaylord that Salmon had the votes to take down the Gingrich speakership, I asked Joe what he would like me to tell Matt.

"Tell him not to do it!" came the hopeless reply. Joe knew through his dealings with myself and others that there was very little that could be said to make conservatives in the Republican Congress ever trust Gingrich again.

In a series of conference calls from his home in Georgia, Gingrich told Republican members that someone else should lead. Irony was thick: House Republicans knew that Gingrich had been moving to the center on taxes and deficits since the government shutdown, while the broader public found him hopelessly out of the mainstream. "We are mourning the loss of not having Newt to kick around anymore," an anonymous Clinton White House adviser told *The Washington Post.* "Newt Gingrich literally was the best thing the Democratic Party has had going for it since 1994. . . . There's total depression on my side of the fence." Later, Karl Rove would tell GOP members that George W. Bush probably would not have won his razor-thin victory over Al Gore in 2000 if he were running on the same ticket as Speaker Gingrich.

The victorious President Clinton saluted his fallen foe.

"Newt Gingrich has been a worthy adversary," Clinton said in a statement. "Despite our profound differences, I appreciate those times we were able to work together in the national interest, especially Speaker Gingrich's strong support for America's continuing leadership for freedom, peace and prosperity in the world." With that, Gingrich, that student of history, returned the dinosaur bones he had borrowed from the Smithsonian for his office and, apparently now a dinosaur himself, brought to a close a moment that was supposed to have been an epoch.

The 1990s ushered in a post-ideological age. Americans now seem to dislike dramatic change whether it's coming from the right or the left. In 1992, Bill Clinton sold himself as a New Democrat. But in 1993 and 1994 President Clinton thought himself a new FDR or LBJ, and paid for it. In 1995 and 1996 Speaker Gingrich and the GOP Congress thought of themselves as the leaders who would finally bring Goldwater conservatism to Washington, and paid for it. "It took about 60 years to erect the modern welfare state," Evan Thomas wrote in *Newsweek* in 1994. "Newt Gingrich wants to dismantle it in a hundred days."

Americans are wary of absolutes and distrust hyperbole. "Since I was a boy, I had watched people assert their piety and moral superiority as justifications for claiming an entitlement to political power, and for demonizing those who begged to differ with them, usually over civil rights," Clinton observed, adding: "Even though I was intrigued by Gingrich and impressed by his political skills, I didn't think much of his claim that his politics represented America's best values." And neither, in the end, did the most conservative members of his own party.

Clinton understood the tides of the time better than the former speaker. "The electorate may be operationally progressive, but philosophically it is moderately conservative and deeply skeptical of government," Clinton wrote in his memoirs. And it was Bill Clinton who never underestimated the Republican presidential nominee in 2000, the man who was challenging Clinton's vice president, Al Gore. In George W. Bush, Clinton knew his VP was staring down a man of great political skill.

12

The Worst of Times

"Big government is not the answer. But the alternative to bureaucracy is not indifference.... This is what I mean by compassionate conservatism."
—*George W. Bush, 2000*

"Now even as we speak, there are those who are preparing to divide us. Well, I say to them tonight, there's not a liberal America and a conservative America; there's the United States of America."
—*Barack Obama, 2004*

FOR ME, ELECTION DAY 2000 BEGAN NORMALLY ENOUGH. I started the day by taking my sons, Joey and Andrew, to school and then dropping by the local diner, the Coffee Cup, to have breakfast and talk over the election with my friends. My own campaign had ended months earlier after I won a heated primary with 79 percent of the vote. (Years later, I am still trying to figure out how I let the other 21 percent get away!) On this sleepy North Florida morning, I was on a ballot unopposed and mentally free to spend the day worrying instead about the presidential race between George W. Bush and Vice President Al Gore.

As voters began streaming toward the polls on that Tuesday in 2000, it felt, to conservatives like myself, as if it had been an eternity since a Republican had occupied the White House. The Clinton years had been packed with one political frustration after another. Governor Clinton's victory over World War II hero George H. W. Bush had been a vertiginous event for those who still wanted to believe that the Reagan coalition of the 1980s would carry the GOP at least through the early years of the twenty-first century. But Clinton's two victories and sky-high approval ratings—even after a flurry of political scandals that began long before his actual impeachment—made it clear, far too late, that winning presidential elections over hapless liberal Democratic candidates was no longer a God-given right.

The new political reality facing the twenty-first-century GOP was shaped by shifting party loyalties, economic disruption, a national Democratic Party made wiser by two decades of defeat, and a level of electoral volatility that defines Washington to this day. George H. W. Bush's loss in 1992 led to Clinton's dominance over the next two years, which led to Newt Gingrich's ascension as speaker two years later, which led to Bill Clinton's reelection in 1996, which ultimately led to Newt Gingrich's departure from town, Bill Clinton's death-defying political survival act, and then, two years after that, a Republican majority and a GOP president. The fact that Newt Gingrich had been replaced in 1998 by a docile Illinois Republican named Denny Hastert temporarily took the harsh edge off the GOP Congress. That George W. Bush was not having to respond to Gingrich gaffes every other day on the campaign trail was a political windfall for Karl Rove and the Bush team. The fact that the 2000 election was so close was simply an indication that the seesaw pattern of the 1990s continued, with Republicans taking both houses of Congress and George W. Bush beating Al Gore to win the White House by the narrowest of margins. The night of that election yielded more drama than any race since John Kennedy inched past Richard Nixon forty years earlier.

Gore began the evening winning a string of states that made his victory seem a foregone conclusion. At 7:50 p.m., the Associated Press called Florida for Gore, forgetting that the most conservative part of the state—where I lived—was in the Central Time Zone, where the polls closed an hour later. It was left to none other than CBS News anchor and longtime GOP whipping boy Dan Rather to tell viewers two hours later that Florida should be taken out of the Gore column and that George W. Bush could still run the table to claim victory.

Over the next few hours, that is exactly what happened, and by the early morning of November 8 my next-door neighbor dropped by to offer a celebratory drink after the networks called the election for Bush. I'm not much for alcohol, but after dealing with Bill Clinton's administration for eight years I immediately grabbed a glass of whiskey and drank it down. We triumphantly declared the end of the Clinton-Gore era. It was 3 a.m. and Al Gore had left his Nashville hotel, en route to War Memorial Plaza to concede the race. I went to bed trying to remember the last time an election result had left me with such a sense of relief.

That relief was short lived. Three hours later I was jolted awake from a phone call from Bush headquarters. Gore had withdrawn his concession and a recount was on.

"We need you in Tallahassee," the voice on the other line said. "Gore's people just dropped a planeload of election lawyers over there and it's about to get ugly." And it did quickly. Bush started the day with a 1,782-vote lead. Within a few days, sixty-four of Florida's sixty-seven counties had recounted their votes and the margin had dropped to 362 votes, based in large part on Democratic challenges. Gore's lawyers fanned quickly across the state and beat the Bush team to the punch. It would make my next thirty-six days spent in Tallahassee, Pensacola, Broward, Miami-Dade, and Palm Beach counties seem like an eternity. George W. Bush ended up winning under all the recount scenarios Al Gore's lawyers presented to the Supreme Court, but that was of little consequence. The Court stepped in, declared Bush the winner, and the man who wanted to be "a uniter, not a divider" began his presidency under a political cloud.

After eight years of peace and prosperity, Bush's narrow win was possible only because the Texas governor consolidated the GOP base early and then moved to the center to attract moderate voters with his promise of a "compassionate conservatism." It was a catchy phrase that was inoffensive to Republicans like myself until he began working to expand the federal education bureaucracy with Massachusetts senator Ted Kennedy while promoting his own brand of big-government Republicanism. The September 11 attacks rallied support behind the president and led to surprising GOP gains in 2002. Over the next few years, George Bush would use that majority to increase domestic and military spending at record rates, while passing a new $7 trillion Medicare entitlement. The deficit was swelling to record levels and Vice President Dick Cheney dismissively told reporters "deficits don't matter."

The ugliness of the Iraq War, the controversy swirling around WMD claims, the horrors of Abu Ghraib, and the mismanagement of U.S. foreign policy should have doomed Bush's reelection efforts. But for all his flaws as a leader, George W. Bush stood firm in his convictions even when much of the evidence undercut his conclusions. Three years after the worst attack ever on American soil, many voters still feared another attack from Islamic terrorists. And enough of those Americans seemed willing to overlook a flawed politician so long as he was a strong leader. Bush played that role well in televised debates as well as inside the Oval Office. His opponent modified his position on the war several times between 2002 and 2004 and, most damningly, was caught on tape telling an audience that he had voted to fund the Iraq War before he voted against it. Bush's success could be explained by Bill Clinton's quote a few years later: "When people are insecure, they'd rather have somebody who is strong and wrong than someone who's weak and right."

Making matters worse for Democratic nominee John Kerry was a bizarre videotape released by al Qaeda's leader. Just as the eleventh-hour surprise of George W. Bush's drunk driving arrest four years earlier had depressed evangelical turnout enough to keep Al Gore in the game, the final weekend of the 2004 campaign saw Osama bin Laden releasing a video calling for the defeat of President Bush. Despite this rather unfortunate "endorsement," Democratic nominee John Kerry seemed to be headed to a sweeping victory as waves of exit polls showed Bush to be a beaten man. By late afternoon, the Massachusetts senator's closest aides were calling him Mr. President and it was left to Karl Rove to tell the sitting president that he might suffer the same fate as his father.

But four years after the recount, Florida rolled in early for Bush, and Democrats were left desperately suggesting that the Bush team had stolen Ohio from Kerry. But that was just a paranoid conspiracy theory pushed by left-wing cable news talk show hosts. Bush had, in fact, beaten the Democrats again, and a deep depression settled over many in the Democratic Party and the national media, who simply could not believe that George W. Bush had won reelection. Many began privately concluding that Karl Rove was right—that the Republican Party might just be headed to a permanent majority, echoing what so many had said in the media forty years earlier about the Democrats, when LBJ won his landslide victory. But like the professional pundits of that era, those buying into Rove's argument would be proven wrong sooner rather than later despite the fact that demographic trends seemed to support his position. After all, George W. Bush had cut heavily into the growing Hispanic vote and carried ninety-seven of the country's hundred fastest-growing counties.

As reporter Timothy Egan explained in *The New York Times*, "You could look out from say, Riverside County, Calif., or Henderson, Nev., to a vast, red-roof-tiled future. New century America was pulling young families and newly middle class immigrants to the far exurbs, creating a vibrant new habitat for the Republican Party."

But a misstep on Social Security, two bloody wars, and a calamitous response to Hurricane Katrina laid waste to Rove's dream of a permanent Republican majority just two years later.

Bush was so remote from Katrina and its destructive aftermath that aides were compelled to put together a DVD of news coverage to school him—you might even say shock him—into realizing that the seeming death by drowning of an American city required real presidential leadership. The Bush excuses—that disaster relief was a local and state matter, or that officials on the ground in the Gulf region had not specifically sought a broader federal role—rang hollow when the federal government in question had had no problem whatever in projecting power across the globe as a matter of choice. Relief in the time of Katrina was a matter of necessity, and the administration's arguments about jurisdictional niceties fell flat. The era of conservative effectiveness that had begun forty years earlier when Democrats could not control the streets of the nation was one of Katrina's victims.

Soon thereafter, Republicans were swept out of the House majority for the first time in a dozen years and San Francisco's Nancy Pelosi became America's first female speaker of the House—and arguably the most liberal speaker in the nation's history. But Pelosi's politics played as insignificant a role in her ascension to the speakership as did Gingrich's twelve years earlier. Two thousand six, like 1994, was about the rejection of a president who was fatally undermined by a partisan agenda and managerial incompetence. The result was disastrous for Rove's Republican Party and an opportunity for Democrats to frame the upcoming 2008 presidential election. The Republican Party and, more important, the conservative movement were in full retreat after years spent as obsequious servants to Bush and Rove's big-government Republicanism. It was a brand of politics that seemed neither compassionate nor conservative to most of the swing voters who decided elections. And those swing voters were to break with the Republicans in both 2008 and 2012.

The contest in 2008 would pivot on a historic Democratic primary process that saw Barack Obama pitted against Hillary Clinton for the future of the party and the country. Obama promised post-partisanship for a deeply divided capital while Senator Clinton mocked the concept as unrealistic.

In early 2008 *The Washington Post* reported that Obama intended to "exploit a deep well of voter revulsion over partisan gridlock in Washington. Sen. Barack Obama is promising to do something that has not been done in modern U.S. politics: unite a coalition of Democrats, Republicans and independents behind an agenda of sweeping change."

Hillary Clinton was openly contemptuous.

"Words are not actions," she said during a Democratic debate in New Hampshire, suggesting that voters put a "reality brake" on her rival's rhetoric. "As beautifully presented and passionately felt as they are," Hillary added, "they are not action."

In pitching himself as a post-partisan politician, though, Obama did manage to assemble a coalition that brought him the nomination, and the White House, aided by a fawning national press corps and the shocking ineptness of the Clinton campaign team.

After his victory, the president-elect met and charmed the most conservative columnists in Washington and even had GOP House majority leader Eric Cantor telling the *Post*'s Bob Woodward that if the new president carried through on his post-partisan promises, he feared the GOP would be in the minority for years.

Cantor needn't have worried. Within days of being sworn in, Obama took to testily telling Republicans visiting the White House that since he won the election, things would go his way. His choice for chief of staff, Rahm Emanuel, was a bare-knuckled partisan who at one point told a reporter that a good crisis should never be wasted. As the American economy seemed to be melting down in 2008, the stimulus plan initially outlined by Obama's economic team was dropped by the White House after liberals on the Hill objected and the GOP members who had once suggested their support could be won backed away after liberals took charge of its drafting. The atmosphere around the Obama team became so partisan, so fast, that retiring New Hampshire Republican Judd Gregg told the White House that he could no longer agree to serve as commerce secretary because of the new administration's sudden, massive jerk to the left.

By August of 2009, conservative and independent voters began joining forces to fight Obama's other big initiative, his health care reform plan. Town hall meetings across America erupted in protests while Democratic politicians faced hostile questioning wherever they went. I remember walking past a TV in my home and seeing the faces of the protesters for the first time. I froze in place staring at people that I recognized so well. They wore Navy caps and patriotic-themed shirts emblazoned with Thomas Jefferson quotes and pictures of the Declaration of Independence. They waved flags that shouted "Don't Tread on Me" while demanding less government and more freedom. They were, in short, the same conservatives that carried me through my first bitterly contested primary against a coalition of country club Republicans and party establishment types. They now had their sights set on Barack Obama's health care plan instead of Bill and Hillary's. But the political outcome was the same.

The Obama White House's intransigence—even after Scott Brown ripped Ted Kennedy's seat out of the Democratic column—eventually led to massive Republican gains in 2010 that could hobble the effectiveness of Barack Obama's administration until he leaves office. Once again in this volatile post-partisan political world, a party lost power only two years after securing what was supposed to be a transformational win at the ballot box. This time, it was the GOP making history as Tea Party–backed candidates helped Republicans win more legislative seats on the national and state levels than any party since the Civil War.

Once again, a president who campaigned as a post-partisan agent of change pandered to his hard-core political base once in office. Bill Clinton promised to be a New Democrat. He wasn't. George W. Bush said he would be a uniter, not a divider. But he created a chasm in politics the likes of which hadn't been seen since Watergate. And Barack Obama promised to bring together Blue and Red State America only to become the most divisive president in the history of modern polling. That is because Barack Obama, like Bill Clinton, sold himself as a post-partisan Democrat and then darted hard left.

Some GOP politicians in Washington made the same mistake. It still boggles my mind that after seeing the failures of Clinton, Bush, Obama, Gingrich, and Pelosi, Republicans would put together a collection of presidential candidates and Senate nominees that would jerk the party's image so far right that they ended up reelecting a Democratic president who had suffered through a miserable debate performance, a listless campaign, and a struggling economy. But that's what happened. Worse, Mitt Romney never fully gained the trust of movement conservatives because he had spent a political career vacillating on political issues much the same way that John McCain had wavered on immigration, and the way that John Kerry had wavered on Iraq. So Republicans had the worst of both worlds in Mitt Romney: a flip-flopping moderate who offended conservatives as well as swing voters when he tried to prove he was "severely conservative."

The political bones of politicians whose careers have been destroyed by hyper-partisanship in this post-partisan age are piled high, from the electoral earthquake of Clinton's victory in 1992 to the Republican revolution of 1994, the Democratic victories of 1998 which made Bill Clinton's party the first since 1844 to pick up congressional seats in a president's second term, the Permanent Majority of 2004, the Pelosi majority of 2006, the Tea Party triumph in 2010, and the reelection of Barack Obama in 2012. Each political earthquake followed an ideological lurch to the left or right. Whether it was Hillarycare or Obamacare, the government shutdown or the Iraq War, politicians in both parties have fed the worst instincts of their most extreme party factions and then paid for it at the voting booth. The volatility that has defined American politics since 1992 will only increase in the coming years because of the disruptions caused by weakened political parties, Internet fund-raising, online organizing, and an ever expanding group of voters who distrust politicians, despise political parties, and hate Washington.

For the Republican Party to survive this new age, it must first recognize it is in this new age. And then it must change—not its timeless values, such as belief in and commitment to limited government, social order, and strength abroad, but rather its short-sighted approach to winning elections and, yes, to governing. Here is how to do it.

Epilogue

The Road to Victory

"We are too great to limit ourselves to small dreams."
—*Ronald Reagan, January 20, 1981*

"THERE IS NO SUBSTITUTE FOR VICTORY"—THE WORDS WERE Douglas MacArthur's—read the sign over the door that led into the makeshift campaign office I set up in my parents' guest bedroom in my first campaign for Congress from northwest Florida in the 1994 cycle. It was written in Magic Marker on a piece of cardboard because that was all the campaign could afford. But it delivered the message that kept me focused on my singular goal in that far-fetched dream. Friends would chuckle as they passed it, knowing that for all my good intentions, I would never beat a sixteen-year Democratic incumbent or a seasoned Republican legislator. One friend examined my ramshackle office and the fury with which I was running my campaign before observing, "You're doing a much better job at this, Joey, than I ever expected. If you keep up this crazy pace, you could finish third or fourth this fall." I smiled, patted him on the back, and thanked him for his generosity.

I would become the first Republican elected in my area in 120 years, and I would win with 62 percent of the vote. Two years later I got 73 percent in my first reelection and in my final congressional campaign, I carried 79 percent of the vote in a primary. By that time, Democrats gave up fielding a candidate against me because I had nailed down my conservative base and worked manically to cut deeply into their own base. I won 50 percent of the vote in most minority precincts. Union members cast their votes for me even if their national leaders had me on a political hit list. Environmentalists found me to be their best conservative friend in Congress because of my work keeping offshore oil drilling away from Florida's Gulf Coast. I argued that even if an accident didn't have a lasting environmental impact, it could ravage family businesses that depended on tourist dollars. Some conservatives in Florida were skeptical (until the BP spill), but they still gave me their vote.

By carrying a 95 percent conservative rating while making strategic alliances with Democratic allies, I boxed out the competition. I also assured myself a place in Congress for the rest of my life if that had been my goal. Because I focused around the clock on building broad coalitions that would also do the nation good, I made sure that I never had to take that General MacArthur quotation down from my parents' upstairs office.

Like all successful politicians and political parties, I did more than parrot my party's political line. I constantly studied the political realities around me and asked what I could do to reach out to those who would not naturally support me. If there were something I could do that would help my constituents, be good for the district, and be consistent with my conservative beliefs, I focused like a laser on getting the job done. And I always tried to remain pragmatic, able to adapt to changing conditions.

History casts an unforgiving eye on political parties that refuse to adapt to changing times. The Whig Party collapsed in the 1850s because it didn't move as a united front against slavery. Republicans were completely irrelevant in national politics for twenty years after Herbert Hoover was blamed for the Great Depression. As we've seen in the previous pages, Democrats were obliterated in five of six presidential elections following the radicalization of their base in 1968. And the Republican Party of our time has lost the popular vote in five of its last six runs for the White House because it continues to run presidential elections based on a faulty understanding of what worked in 1988. Even GOP operatives believe America elected George H. W. Bush because of flags and furloughs. Flags and furloughs played their part, yes, but there was more to it than Atwater's strategy and tactics. Americans chose the first President Bush in part for the same reasons they chose Eisenhower, Nixon, and Reagan: they believed him to be a realistic leader in touch with mainstream values—a candidate who, despite popular caricatures, would govern largely from the middle of the political spectrum rather than its fringes.

The national Republican Party will continue its collapse unless leaders, activists, and primary voters embrace again Bill Buckley's view that "conservatism, except when it is expressed in pure idealism, takes into account reality." Had the party followed Buckley's advice and supported the most electable conservatives instead of the most ideologically extreme in recent cycles, Republicans would now control the United States Senate and Democratic leader Harry Reid would be in retirement in Nevada.

For the GOP to win again, it must take Buckley's ruthlessly pragmatic approach to primary elections and seek out conservative candidates who can win sweeping majorities by holding down their base and thus close the deal on carrying swing districts in critical states. That means we have to stop electing amateurs in primaries who serve as little more than ideological indulgences, who exploit resentments that play well enough among the base, but whose positions make them nonviable in general elections.

Buckley himself grew more realistic and shrewd politically after experiencing firsthand the collapse of Barry Goldwater in 1964 and the election of Ronald Reagan as governor of California two years later. That is why the *National Review* founder never forgot that beating liberal Democrats sometimes requires voting for Republicans who are more moderate temperamentally, ideologically, or both. Republicans lost the White House and U.S. Senate not because of any irreversible sociological trend but because GOP voters in presidential primaries, as well as in the campaigns of Republicans like Todd Akin, Richard Mourdock, Christine O'Donnell, and Sharron Angle, were more interested in indulging their Republican resentments than they were in electing a candidate who could win in the fall.

Taking a winning, pragmatic approach has not come naturally to me. My first few years in Congress were spent at war with moderates in my own party as much as liberals in the Democratic Party. I saw the more moderate members from outside the Deep South as enemies of the bigger cause. That changed in 1998 when Oklahoma congressman Steve Largent led a small group of conservatives to campaign for candidates in swing districts across the Northeast, Midwest, and Pacific Northwest. Watching these Republicans campaign for their lives in states like Illinois, Oregon, and Washington, where the political punch lines of the Reagan years drew little more

than polite applause, made me realize that instead of being my political adversaries, these Republicans were the reason I was in the
majority party in Congress. I had learned that from Steve Largent, a
soft-spoken man but an uncompromising conservative, who also
taught me that a winning temperament often offsets an ideology
that would be unacceptable in other candidates. Of all the Republicans I have met in Washington over the past twenty years, none possessed more Reagan-like qualities than Steve Largent. I have long
considered his defeat in 2002 to be a great loss not only for the Republican Party but also for America. While he may not have possessed all the skills of Ronald Reagan, his humble tone and moderate
temperament were a perfect complement to his conservative philosophy.

Before that formative experience, I remember speaking out
against the possibility of Colin Powell's presidential candidacy in 1996
because his political moderation was so off-putting to me. The
thought that he could be the standard-bearer of my Republican Party
was offensive. But watching the retired general on *Meet the Press*
in recent years has made me understand why Ronald Reagan and
George H. W. Bush drafted him to be a critical player in their administrations. It also made me realize in retrospect how much better
the GOP would have fared against Bill Clinton in 1996 if I had not let
my hopes for a conservative stalwart get in the way of our best hope to
beat Clinton while making history. "If it's just going to represent the
far right wing of the political spectrum, I think the party is in difficulty," said Powell. "I'm a moderate, but I'm still a Republican."

This war hero, who had made history of his own by becoming the
first African American chairman of the Joint Chiefs of Staff and secretary of state, should still be one of the leading voices in the Repub-

lican Party *because* of, not in spite of, his centrist political philosophy. The need for moderates like General Powell is especially urgent since the GOP faces the most daunting of demographic trends.

While George W. Bush may have carried most of America's fastest-growing counties eight years earlier, the crushing defeat Mitt Romney experienced in 2012 at the hands of African Americans, Hispanic voters, Asian Americans, and most other minorities made gains in those counties of little value. Despite the desperate need to have GOP leaders who offer a more diverse look and approach, Powell is a pariah in his own party, a relic from an age when the Republican Party had two wings and could win forty-nine out of fifty states. To not only call for the toleration of a moderate wing but to define it as necessary may offend some conservative extremists, but it does not offend me. I like to win and I like to win big. A shrinking GOP base will never by itself achieve the type of landslides that Ike and Reagan each put together twice.

Republicans can kick moderates like General Powell out of its party's mainstream and drive them into the arms of the Democratic Party every four years, or they can leave their ideological comfort zone, work aggressively to expand their political coalitions, and start stealing swing voters away from Democrats like Hillary Clinton. Unfortunately, the Republican Party of the moment bears little resemblance to the party of Ronald Reagan, who would have responded to Powell's critiques of the Republican Party with an all-hands-on-deck effort to win the war hero back. That's because President Reagan lived by the belief that "just because I'm your friend 80 percent of the time doesn't make me your enemy 20 percent of the time."

Powell has been aligned with Republican ideas for decades. His positions on the economy fit comfortably in the mainstream of American conservative thought. "Everything I observe affirms my belief in free enterprise," said Powell. "It creates new wealth, generates new jobs, enables people to live good lives, fuels demand, and triggers fresh enterprise, starting the cycle all over again. Government should not interfere with the demonstrated success of the free marketplace, beyond controls to protect public safety and to prevent distortions of competition by either labor or industry."

On education, Powell has long supported tough reforms, the testing of teachers, charter schools, vouchers, and the promotion of homeschooling long before such reforms became in vogue. The general summed up his position by saying, "Let's use innovation and competition, good old American innovation, good old American competition to help give our children the best education possible."

Powell's position on foreign policy is much more in line with the GOP's long tradition of realism than the stance of those who have seemed to propose military adventurism at every turn over the past decade. While I am far closer to General Powell's view of foreign policy than John McCain's, I believe a vibrant and growing Republican Party would be served best by having both neoconservatives and realists under their big tent. The same holds true for social conservatives and political moderates who take a more libertarian view on issues like abortion and gay marriage.

This may come as a shock to certain ideology- (and profit-) driven talk radio hosts who unleash fury at anyone who disagrees with them on a few issues, but parties win the White House by nominating candidates who win the most votes—not feeding endlessly on base resentments that offend crossover voters and shrink the GOP's voter rolls.

If the Republican Party is big enough to reach out to disaffected moderates like Colin Powell, then it will be big enough to win the White House in 2016, even if Hillary Clinton is the Democratic nominee. The question is whether the GOP will choose to go the way of William F. Buckley or Glenn Beck.

The survival of our party depends on that choice. And because I believe in reducing the federal government's reach, expanding personal freedoms, reforming regulations, balancing the budget, ending foreign adventures, nominating conservative justices, and keeping tax rates as low as possible, I believe that America's success depends upon a strong Republican Party. Democrats obviously disagree, and will continue their fight for bigger government, higher taxes, more regulations, and the appointment of liberal justices. The only way to stop liberals from continuing their winning streak in the White House is by pulling in moderates, independents, and swing voters who have been driven into the Democrats' camp because of Washington Republicans' narrowing vision.

We can win again and we will. And we can do it by following the right paths of Ronald Reagan and Dwight Eisenhower. We can do it by fighting for the core principles of conservatism and emphasizing those values that most Americans agree with. There will also be times when we will follow the lead of Reagan and Eisenhower by putting principled pragmatism before ideological battles that will undermine our ability to win elections, elect majorities, and take back control of the White House. But time is wasting. Hillary Clinton's supporters are already preparing for political battle. Next time, we'd better be prepared to win. There is no substitute for victory, and I for one am damn tired of my party losing presidential elections.

Acknowledgments

I am grateful to my *Morning Joe* team, starting, of course, with Mika and Phil Griffin. I so appreciate their friendship and encouragement over the past year. Jon Meacham's invaluable contributions made this book possible. Thanks as well to Will Murphy, Gina Centrello, Susan Kamil, and Tom Perry, who help Jon run a fantastic publishing team at Random House—I thank them for their support and confidence. Thanks, too, to Mika Kasuga, London King, and Dennis Ambrose. Bill Kristol, Tom Brokaw, Doris Kearns Goodwin, Craig Shirley, and Michael Beschloss were generous early readers. Louis Burgdorf was, and is, irreplaceable. And I am so grateful for my family, especially the four wonderful children to whom this book is dedicated.

Some Notes on the Sources

LIKE MANY OF YOU, I'M AN UNABASHED FAN OF GREAT PO-litical biography and historical narratives. The sources listed below are not exhaustive, but I hope they acknowledge my debt to the writers and scholars whose work has informed my own look back. Books by Theodore H. White, William F. Buckley, Jr., Russell Kirk, Craig Shirley, Rick Perlstein, Sam Tanenhaus, Steven Hayward, William Manchester, and Lou Cannon have been particularly important in my thinking about America from World War II forward, and where the Republicans stood yesterday. As careful readers will probably note, this book takes a shift in tone from historical essay and more toward personal history beginning in the early 1990s, when my own active involvement in politics began. That's for obvious reasons, and I think reflects my passion for the present and the future—both of which are deeply rooted in the past, but which, unlike history, remain bendable to our purposes, if only we have the good sense and the practical skill to make it so.

Foreword

xi   **"It was invisible, as always":** White, *Making of the President 1960*, 3.

xiii   **Lionel Trilling suggested:** The observation is from Trilling's 1950 book, *The Liberal Imagination*. For the quotation and analysis from a conservative perspective, see http://www.firstthings.com/blogs /firstthoughts/2010/12/21/liberalism-and-irritable-mental-gestures.

1: A Dislike for Ike

I have drawn on the memoirs of the key figures discussed in this chapter—chiefly books by Truman, Eisenhower, and Nixon. Rick Perlstein's *Before the Storm* informed my thinking, too, as did Sam Tanenhaus's work on Whittaker Chambers and on conservatism itself. Also essential, of course, were the standard biographies of the central characters, from James MacGregor Burns on FDR to David McCullough's portrait of Truman to Stephen E. Ambrose's multivolume works on Eisenhower and Nixon.

3   **"Should any political party"**: Gould, *Grand Old Party*, 335–36.

3   **"It stands athwart history"**: http://www.nationalreview.com /articles/223549/our-mission-statement/william-f-buckley-jr.

4   **Over lunch:** Ambrose, *Eisenhower*, I, 515.

4   **At Potsdam in 1945:** McCullough, *Truman*, 429–30.

4   **"You can't join a party"**: *The New York Times*, November 7, 1951.

5   **"The measures undertaken"**: Gould, *Grand Old Party*, 268.

6   **"This active inactivity"**: http://www.whitehouse.gov/about /presidents/calvincoolidge.

7   **"modern American conservatism largely organized itself"**: Kabaservice, *Rule and Ruin*, 13–14.

8   **"padlock the state treasury"**: Tanenhaus, *Death of Conservatism*, 84.

9   **Buckley struck out against Yale:** Ibid., 49.

9   **Buckley's purpose, Wills recalled:** Wills, *Confessions of a Conservative*, 4.

10   **"We could not have found"**: Sherwood, *Roosevelt and Hopkins*, 847.

10   **"We really believed"**: Ibid., 870.

12   **In California's 12th Congressional District:** I drew on Nixon's memoirs and the first volume of Ambrose's Nixon biography for this account of Nixon's political beginnings.

12   **"One advocated by the New Deal"**: Ambrose, *Nixon*, I, 120.

13   **"REMEMBER," said a Nixon ad:** Ibid., 137.

13   **On the eve of the general election:** Ibid., 138.

15   **the ticket of Ike and Dick:** Jeffrey Frank's good book on the relationship between the two men, *Ike and Dick*, is instructive.

16   a president is like "the commander of a ship": This observation of Henry Adams's has been popularized in our day by Arthur Schlesinger, Jr. For Schlesinger's best-known use of the quotation, see http://potus-geeks.livejournal.com/250623.html.

17   Eisenhower has long been the subject of historical revisionism: Evan Thomas's *Ike's Bluff: President Eisenhower's Secret Battle to Save the World*, a fresh look at Eisenhower's abhorrence of the possibility of nuclear conflict, is the latest and best example of the trend begun by Greenstein.

18   "There will be an immediate & radical revision": Donovan, *Eisenhower: The Inside Story*, 55.

20   "Our industrial plant is built": Eisenhower, *Mandate for Change*, 120–21.

20   "I did not share the belief": Ibid., 121.

20   "In initiating a reversal of trends": Ibid.

20   Eisenhower was unwilling to sacrifice reality to ideology: This account of the $70 billion episode with Taft is drawn from ibid., 131.

22   "It seemed that almost every day": Ibid., 320.

23   There was the emergence of the ultraright John Birch Society: Perlstein, *Before the Storm*, 110.

23   "The New Deal, Dean Acheson wrote approvingly": Goldwater, *Conscience of a Conservative*, 9.

24   "Here we have": Ibid., 9–14.

2: Between a Rock and the Right

26   "I do not undertake to promote welfare": Goldwater, *Conscience of a Conservative*, 17.

26   "The only answer to a strategy of victory": http://www.presidency.ucsb.edu/ws/?pid=25974.

26   Tom Dewey had some advice: Nixon, *RN*, 199.

27   "In the end": Ibid.

28   "My campaigning had had": Ibid., 200.

28   Nixon adjourned for a strategy session: White, *Making of the President 1960*, 62–63.

29   "I've never found it a handicap": Ibid., 66.

32   "I hate the thought": Ibid., 71.

32   **young aide named John Ehrlichman:** Ambrose, *Nixon*, I, 539.

32   **"My friend, you have":** Perlstein, *Before the Storm*, 20–21.

33   **In April 1957 the senator was asked to lunch:** "Republicans: Now the Republicans Rumble," *Time*, April 22, 1957.

33   **"siren song of socialism":** Ibid.

34   **"There is something perhaps especially Californian":** White, *Making of the President 1960*, 65.

34   **"These people liked Ike":** Ibid., 74.

35   **"A new period now begins":** Ibid., 184.

36   **"If we weren't concerned with winning":** "Republicans: The Bold Stroke," *Time*, August 1, 1960.

37   **The key to that support:** Ibid.

37   **secretly boarded a plane in Washington:** Ibid.

37   **Nixon had asked Eisenhower for help:** Ambrose, *Nixon*, I, 547.

37   **"I restated my position":** "Republicans: The Bold Stroke," *Time*, August 1, 1960.

37   **Nixon stayed in the Rockefeller wing and region:** "Republicans: The Men Who . . . ," *Time*, August 8, 1960.

38   **Hours passed and Rockefeller bombarded Nixon:** White, *Making of the President 1960*, 388–89.

39   **"If you don't think":** "Republicans: The Bold Stroke."

39   **Ike was deeply insulted:** Ibid.

39   **"damned sellout":** Ibid.

39   **"I think the Republican Party":** Perlstein, *Before the Storm*, 85.

39   **After the Compact of Fifth Avenue:** Ambrose, *Nixon*, I, 552.

39   **"What I'm trying to do":** Ibid.

40   **"The United States can and must":** Ibid.

40   *Time* **approved of Nixon's kowtowing:** "Republicans: The Bold Stroke," *Time*, August 1, 1960.

41   **Goldwater put away his talk of Munich:** Perlstein, *Before the Storm*, 94.

42   **in favor of Barry Goldwater for president:** White, *Making of the President 1960*, 206.

42   **After John Kennedy's inaugural ceremonies:** Nixon, *RN*, 227–28.

3: Goldwater, Extremism, and the Rise of LBJ

Perlstein, *Before the Storm*, and Manchester, *The Glory and the Dream*, are revealing accounts of the rising tensions and dramas of the mid-1960s.

44 **"The election of 1960":** White, *Making of the President 1964*, 64.

49 **Richard Nixon had carried 32 percent of the African American vote:** And he won 18 percent in 1972.

50 **"I will not cede more power to the state":** http://www.nytimes.com /books/00/07/16/specials/buckley-liberalism.html.

52 **"I wanted them to spend two days":** White, *Making of the President 1964*, 97.

52 **the campaign for the Republican nomination:** Ibid., 118.

53 **"it's still a free country":** Ibid., 211–12.

53 **President Eisenhower's speech to the delegates:** Ibid., 210.

54 **"The Good Lord raised this mighty Republic":** Ibid., 227–28.

54 **"My God, he's going to run as Barry Goldwater":** Ibid., 228.

54 **"I would like the Governor":** *The New York Times*, July 17, 1964.

55 **"no immediate plans":** Ibid.

56 **"In his drive for the nomination":** *The Atlantic Monthly*, October 1, 1964.

57 **"Barry Goldwater not only lost":** Perlstein, *Before the Storm*, 513.

57 **"The paranoid spokesman sees":** *Harper's*, October 1964.

4: Reagan's Rendezvous with Destiny

The rise of Reagan is the subject of a growing number of great books. I found Matthew Dallek's *The Right Moment* particularly valuable, as well as Reagan's own 1965 memoir, *Where's the Rest of Me?* Lou Cannon, who covered Reagan for *The Washington Post*, remains the Homeric chronicler of all things Reagan.

60 **"You know I'm running against an actor":** Dallek, *Right Moment*, 235.

60 **"Today, more than ever":** Reagan, *Where's the Rest of Me?*, 300.

60   "Thank you": The text of "The Speech" is widely available online; I also recommend watching the video of the address.

68   **In a joint appearance at the National Negro Republican Assembly:** Cannon, *Reagan*, 111.

69   **"In a clear departure":** Dallek, *Right Moment*, 195.

70   **"We do have the party glued together":** Ibid., 216.

70   **"There isn't anything we can't do":** Ibid., 237.

71   **"Reagan was underestimated":** Cannon, *Reagan*, 118.

72   **distant but not unrealistic hope:** Ibid., 160.

74   Teddy White was to invoke: White, *Making of the President 1968*, 47.

5: The Lift of a Driving Dream

75   **"Bring Us Together":** *The New York Times*, November 8, 1968.

75   **"We cannot learn from one another":** http://www.bartleby.com /124/pres58.html.

75   **When Richard Nixon was weighing:** Nixon, *RN*, 292.

75   **Nixon also sought counsel from Billy Graham:** Ibid., 292–93.

76   **"Gentlemen, this is *not*":** Ibid., 297.

76   **"neither a conservative nor a liberal":** White, *Making of the President 1968*, 148.

76   **"lift of a driving dream":** Reeves, *President Nixon*, 294.

77   **"We are not here to accuse":** *The New York Times*, August 5, 1968.

77   **"different from the old voices":** White, *Making of the President 1968*, 379.

78   **reporting on a Nixon Southern stop:** Ibid., 380.

79   **"There is no way":** http://www.guardian.co.uk/world/2005/feb/21 /books.usa.

80   **"There's been a lot":** McGinniss, *Selling of the President 1968*, 21.

82   **Nixon noticed a poster:** Nixon, *RN*, 330.

82   **"a lot more fun":** Ibid., 335.

82   **"We seek an open world":** http://www.bartleby.com/124/pres58 .html.

82   **"There certainly is a new Nixon":** McGinniss, *Selling of the President 1968*, 70.

84 "The liberal Eastern establishment": Tanenhaus, *Death of Conservatism*, 89.

85 "A raised eyebrow": http://www.americanrhetoric.com/speeches /spiroagnewtvnewscoverage.htm.

86 "He felt that newspapermen": Nixon, *RN*, 432.

86 "Don't promise more": Ibid., 353.

87 "The country recognizes": Ibid., 414.

6: Acid, Amnesty, and Abortion

88 "You fellows just don't know McGovern": Nixon, *RN*, 657.

88 "Let me just read you a letter": Ibid., 673.

89 "had consciously abandoned": Ibid., 657.

90 "The Eastern Establishment media": Reeves, *President Nixon*, 498.

90 Officials in the president's reelection campaign: Ibid., 517.

90 the New Majority was formed: http://www.creators.com/opinion /pat-buchanan/who-killed-the-new-majority.html.

90 Nixon took time to sit down with Teddy White: White, *Making of the President 1972*, 10.

91 "I was ready to take a stand": Nixon, *RN*, 354.

93 "We even deliberated for several days": Ibid., 769.

93 "The 'Connally for President' discussion": http://articles.baltimore sun.com/1994-05-20/news/1994140195_1_connally-nixon-new -party.

94 "Had a long session with Connally": Ibid.

95 "We have passed through": Reeves, *President Nixon*, 543–44.

7: The Dream Is Still with Us

98 "I believe the Republican Party": Cannon, *Governor Reagan*, 401.

98 "You got me out, you sons of bitches": Ford, *A Time to Heal*, 345.

99 "RN feels that Ronald Reagan": http://www.fordlibrarymuseum .gov/library/exhibits/campaign/016800303-001.pdf.

99 "Regardless of whether": http://www.ford.utexas.edu/library /exhibits/campaign/005601363-005.pdf.

99   "His general ignorance of national affairs": http://www.fordlibrary
      museum.gov/library/exhibits/campaign/020401482-001.pdf.

99   "Gerry Ford is so dumb": http://www.guardian.co.uk/world/2006
      /99/27/guardianobituaries.usa.

101   suggested that a corrupt bargain with Nixon: http://news.google
      .com/newspapers?nid=1314&dat=19751218&id=EfBLAAAAIBAJ
      &sjid=c-0DAAAAIBAJ&pg=2338,1088253.

103   the "challenge from the right": Ford, *A Time to Heal*, 333–34.

104   "I happen to believe": Cannon, *Reagan*, 194.

105   "Now, I hope and pray": Ibid., 195.

105   creating a new conservative party: Ibid., 197.

106   offer Reagan the Commerce Department: Ibid., 199.

106   "The '72 election gave us a new majority": Ibid., 198.

107   "When you vote Tuesday": Ibid., 220.

107   "We don't want a repetition": Ford, *A Time to Heal*, 389.

107   "You are the President": Barry Goldwater to Gerald Ford, May 7,
      1976, Gerald R. Ford Presidential Library and Museum.

107   President Ford had a narrow delegate lead: Ford, *A Time to Heal*,
      220–21.

107   "This is a pitiful little party": "Republicans: Now the Republicans
      Rumble," *Time*, May 17, 1976.

108   "We just got the best news": Ford, *A Time to Heal*, 394.

110   the former California governor quoted a poet: Cannon, *Reagan*,
      226.

110   "We are at peace with ourselves": Reagan, *A Life in Letters*, 222.

8: A New Hope

111   "A recession is when": http://www.reagan.utexas.edu/archives
      /reference/9.1.80.html.

112   "Riding point leaves you pretty exposed": Reagan, *A Life in Letters*,
      233.

114   "I know that in speaking to this crowd": http://neshobademocrat
      .com/main.asp?SectionID=2&SubSectionID=297&Article
      ID=15599.

114   "Eight million out of work": http://www.reagan.utexas.edu
      /archives/reference/9.1.80.html.

116 Even Richard Wirthlin, Reagan's pollster: Cannon, *Reagan*, 269.
117 Later in the fall Carter said outright: Ibid., 283.
118 "You'll determine whether or not": Ibid., 284.

9: You Ain't Seen Nothing Yet

120 "As an individual you incarnate": Buckley, *Let Us Talk of Many Things*, 322.
120 "Let us be sure": http://reagan2020.us/speeches/state_of_the _union_1984.asp.
120 the kind of coverage *Time* magazine gave Ronald Reagan: *Time*, July 7, 1986.
125 "With the right to bear arms": *The New York Times*, March 29, 1981.
125 a National Rifle Association official: Ibid.
125 "This is a matter of vital importance": http://articles.latimes .com/1994-05-05/news/mn-54185_1_assault-weapons-ban/2.
126 In 1985, at the thirtieth anniversary dinner for *National Review*: *Newsweek*, October 17, 2008.

10: The Polo Populist

128 "I do not hate government": http://www.presidency.ucsb.edu /ws/?pid=25955.
128 "He came out and gave me a Snickers": Brady, *Bad Boy*, 9.
131 "I think conservatives in general": http://www.thedailybeast.com /articles/2013/03/05/newt-gingrich-faces-reality-admits -conservatives-were-out-of-touch.html.
135 "Although [Bush] still led": Clinton, *My Life*, 392.
138 "It was beginning to sink in": *The New York Times*, November 4, 1992.

11: A Revolution Unravels

139 "We will build an American community": http://www.presidency .ucsb.edu/ws/?pid=25958.
139 "There is a Democratic Party": http://www.c-spanvideo.org /program/31300-1.

141   "The Reagan failure was to grossly undervalue": http://articles
       .washingtonpost.com/2012-02-19/politics/35442043_1_gingrich
       -aide-frank-gregorsky-newt-gingrich.

142   "When I say save the West, I mean that": Ibid.

142   "I have enormous personal ambition": http://www.pbs.org/wgbh
       /pages/frontline/newt/vanityfair1.html.

143   "counterculture McGovernicks": Clinton, *My Life*, 633.

148   "The atmosphere of hostility": Ibid., 651.

148   "a slow but inexorable": Ibid., 654.

149   "I melt when I'm around him": *Newsweek*, August 18, 1996.

149   After a joint town hall meeting: Clinton, *My Life*, 659.

150   "Of course there were": Ibid., 634.

155   "Since I was a boy": Ibid., 633.

155   "The electorate may be operationally progressive": Ibid., 632.

12: The Worst of Times

156   "Big government is not the answer": http://www.presidency.ucsb
       .edu/ws/?pid=25954.

156   "Now even as we speak": http://www.washingtonpost.com/wp
       -dyn/articles/A19751-2004Jul27.html.

161   "You could look out": http://campaignstops.blogs.nytimes.com
       /2012/04/17/the-impermanent-republican-majority/.

163   "exploit a deep well": http://www.washingtonpost.com/wp-dyn
       /content/article/2008/01/06/AR2008010602402.html.

163   "Words are not actions": Ibid.

Bibliography

Books

Ambrose, Stephen E. *Eisenhower, Vol. 1: Soldier, General of the Army, President-Elect, 1890–1952*. New York: Simon & Schuster, 1983.

———. *Eisenhower, Vol. 2: The President*. New York: Simon & Schuster, 1984.

———. *Nixon, Vol. 1: The Education of a Politician 1913–1962*. New York: Simon & Schuster, 1987.

———. *Nixon, Vol. 2: The Triumph of a Politician 1962–1972*. New York: Simon & Schuster, 1989.

———. *Nixon, Vol. 3: Ruin and Recovery, 1973–1990*. New York: Simon & Schuster, 1991.

Brady, John. *Bad Boy: The Life and Politics of Lee Atwater*. Cambridge: Da Capo, 1996.

Buchanan, Patrick J. *Right from the Beginning*. Washington, D.C.: Regnery, 1990.

Buckley, William F., Jr. *God and Man at Yale: The Superstitions of "Academic Freedom."* Washington, D.C.: Regnery, 1986.

———. *Let Us Talk of Many Things: The Collected Speeches*. New York: Crown, 2000.

———. *Miles Gone By: A Literary Autobiography*. Washington, D.C.: Regnery, 2005.

———. *Up from Liberalism*. New York: Stein & Day, 1984.

Burns, James MacGregor. *Roosevelt, Vol. 1: The Lion and the Fox, 1882–1940*. New York: Houghton Mifflin Harcourt, 2003.

———. *Roosevelt, Vol. 2: The Soldier of Freedom, 1940–1945*. New York: Harcourt Brace Jovanovich, 1970.

Bush, George H. W. *All the Best, George Bush: My Life in Letters and Other Writings.* New York: Touchstone, 2000.

Bush, George W., and Karen Hughes. *A Charge to Keep.* New York: William Morrow, 1999.

———. *Decision Points.* New York: Crown, 2010.

Cannon, Lou. *Governor Reagan: His Rise to Power.* New York: PublicAffairs, 2003.

———. *President Reagan: The Role of a Lifetime.* New York: Simon & Schuster, 1991.

———. *Reagan.* New York: G. P. Putnam's Sons, 1982.

Carter, Jimmy. *Keeping Faith: Memoirs of a President.* Fayetteville: University of Arkansas Press, 1995.

Cheney, Dick, and Liz Cheney. *In My Time: A Personal and Political Memoir.* New York: Threshold, 2011.

Clinton, Bill. *My Life.* New York: Knopf, 2004.

Dallek, Matthew. *The Right Moment: Ronald Reagan's First Victory and the Decisive Turning Point in American Politics.* New York: Free Press, 2000.

Donovan, Robert J. *Eisenhower: The Inside Story.* New York: Harper & Brothers, 1956.

Eisenhower, Dwight D. *Mandate for Change, 1953–1956: The White House Years.* New York: Doubleday, 1963.

———. *Waging Peace, 1956–1961: The White House Years.* New York: Doubleday, 1965.

Ford, Gerald R. *A Time to Heal: The Autobiography of Gerald R. Ford.* New York: Harper & Row, 1979.

Frank, Jeffrey. *Ike and Dick: Portrait of a Strange Political Marriage.* New York: Simon & Schuster, 2013.

Gingrich, Newt. *To Renew America.* New York: HarperCollins, 1996.

Goldwater, Barry. *The Conscience of a Conservative.* Princeton, N.J.: Princeton University Press, 2007.

———. *Why Not Victory? A Fresh Look at American Foreign Policy.* New York: McGraw-Hill, 1962.

Gould, Lewis L. *Grand Old Party: A History of the Republicans.* New York: Oxford University Press, 2012.

Greenstein, Fred I. *The Hidden-Hand Presidency: Eisenhower as Leader.* Baltimore: Johns Hopkins University Press, 1994.

Haldeman, H. R. *The Haldeman Diaries: Inside the Nixon White House.* New York: Penguin, 1994.

Hayward, Steven F. *The Age of Reagan, 1964–1980: The Fall of the Old Liberal Order.* New York: Crown, 2001.

Kabaservice, Geoffrey. *Rule and Ruin: The Downfall of Moderation and the Destruction of the Republican Party, from Eisenhower to the Tea Party.* New York: Oxford University Press, 2012.

Kirk, Russell. *The Conservative Mind: From Burke to Eliot.* Washington, D.C.: Regnery, 2001.

Larson, Arthur. *A Republican Looks at His Party.* London: Greenwood, 1974.

Manchester, William. *The Glory and the Dream: A Narrative History of America, 1932–1972.* New York: Random House, 1984.

McCullough, David. *Truman.* New York: Simon & Schuster, 1992.

McGinniss, Joe. *The Selling of the President 1968.* New York: Simon & Schuster, 1969.

Meacham, Jon. *American Lion: Andrew Jackson in the White House.* New York: Random House, 2008.

Nixon, Richard. *RN: The Memoirs of Richard Nixon.* New York: Simon & Schuster, 1990.

Perlstein, Rick. *Before the Storm: Barry Goldwater and the Unmaking of the American Consensus.* New York: Nation Books, 2001.

———. *Nixonland: The Rise of a President and the Fracturing of America.* New York: Scribner, 2008.

Reagan, Ronald. *An American Life: The Autobiography.* New York: Simon & Schuster, 1990.

———. *Reagan: A Life in Letters.* New York: Free Press, 2004.

———. *Where's the Rest of Me? The Autobiography of Ronald Reagan.* New York: Karz, 1981.

Reeves, Richard. *President Nixon: Alone in the White House.* New York: Touchstone, 2001.

———. *President Reagan: The Triumph of Imagination.* New York: Simon & Schuster, 2005.

Regnery, Alfred S. *Upstream: The Ascendance of American Conservatism.* New York: Threshold, 2008.

Schlesinger, Arthur M., Jr. *The Imperial Presidency.* New York: Mariner, 2004.

Sherwood, Robert E. *Roosevelt and Hopkins: An Intimate History.* New York: Enigma, 2008.

Shirley, Craig. *Rendezvous with Destiny: Ronald Reagan and the Campaign That Changed America.* Wilmington, Del.: ISI, 2009.

Skinner, Kiron K., Annelise Anderson, and Martin Anderson, eds. *Reagan: A Life in Letters.* New York: Free Press, 2003.

Smith, Jean Edward. *Eisenhower in War and Peace.* New York: Random House, 2012.

Tanenhaus, Sam. *The Death of Conservatism.* New York: Random House, 2009.

———. *Whittaker Chambers: A Biography.* New York: Random House, 1997.

Thomas, Evan. *Ike's Bluff: President Eisenhower's Secret Battle to Save the World.* New York: Little, Brown, 2012.

Trilling, Lionel. *The Liberal Imagination.* New York: New York Review of Books, 2008.

White, Theodore H. *The Making of the President 1960.* New York: Harper Perennial Political Classics, 2009.

———. *The Making of the President 1964.* New York: Harper Perennial Political Classics, 2010.

———. *The Making of the President 1968.* New York: Harper Perennial Political Classics, 2010.

———. *The Making of the President 1972.* New York: Harper Perennial Political Classics, 2010.

Wills, Garry. *Confessions of a Conservative.* New York: Penguin, 1980.

Periodicals

Buckley, William F., Jr. "Our Mission Statement." *National Review,* November 19, 1955. http://www.nationalreview.com/articles/223549/our-mission-statement/william-f-buckley-jr.

———. "The Waning of the GOP." *National Review,* April 28, 2007. http://www.nationalreview.com/articles/220761/waning-gop/william-f-buckley-jr.

Dowd, Maureen. "The 1992 Elections: Disappointment—Road to Defeat: Sifting Strategies: What Went Wrong, and Right; Bush: As the Loss Sinks In, Some Begin Pointing Fingers." *The New York Times,* November 5, 1992. http://www.nytimes.com/1992/11/05/us/1992

-elections-disappointment-road-defeat-sifting-strategies-what-went
-wrong.html?pagewanted=all&src=pm.

Eaton, William J. "Ford, Carter, Reagan Push for Gun Ban." *Los Angeles Times*, May 5, 1994. http://articles.latimes.com/1994-05-05/news /mn-54185_1_assault-weapons-ban/2.

Egan, Timothy. "The Impermanent Republican Majority." Campaign Stops Blog *(The New York Times)*, April 17, 2012. http://campaign stops.blogs.nytimes.com/2012/04/17/the-impermanent -republican-majority/.

Germond, Jack, and Jules Witcover. "Connally Awed Nixon, as Halde-man Diaries Tell." *The Baltimore Sun*, May 20, 1994. http://articles .baltimoresun.com/1994-05-20/news/1994140195_1_connally -nixon-new-party.

Hofstadter, Richard. "The Paranoid Style in American Politics." *Harper's*, October 1964, 77–86.

Holmes, Steven A. "Gun Control Bill Backed by Reagan in Appeal to Bush." *The New York Times*, March 29, 1981. http://www.nytimes .com/1991/03/29/us/gun-control-bill-backed-by-reagan-in-appeal -to-bush.html.

"Hunter S. Thompson Dies at 67." *The Guardian*, February 21, 2005. http://www.guardian.co.uk/world/2005/feb/21/books.usa.

Jackson, Harold. "Obituary: Gerald Ford." *The Guardian*, December 27, 2006.   http://www.guardian.co.uk/world/2006/dec/27/guardian obituaries.usa.

Krock, Arthur. *The New York Times*, November 7, 1951.

Markon, Jerry. "Gingrich Archives Show His Public Praise, Private Criti-cism of Reagan." *The Washington Post*, February 19, 2012. http://articles.washingtonpost.com/2012-02-19/politics/35442043 _1_gingrich-aide-frank-gregorsky-newt-gingrich.

Meacham, Jon. "It's Not Easy Bein' Blue." *Newsweek*, October 17, 2008. http://www.thedailybeast.com/newsweek/2008/10/17/it-s-not-easy -bein-blue.html.

Mohr, Charles. "Goldwater View Is 'Frightening' to Rockefeller." *The New York Times*, July 18, 1964. http://www.nytimes.com/learning /general/specials/elections/1964/featured_article1.html.

Morrow, Lance. "Ronald Reagan: Yankee Doodle Magic." *Time*, July 7, 1986.   http://www.time.com/time/magazine/article/0,9171,961668, 00.html.

"Republicans: Now the Republicans Rumble." *Time*, May 17, 1976. http://www.time.com/time/magazine/article/0,9171,945591,00.html.

"Republicans: The Backward Look." *Time*, April 22, 1957. http://www.time.com/time/magazine/article/0,9171,824782,00.html.

"Republicans: The Bold Stroke." *Time*, August 1, 1960. http://www.time.com/time/magazine/article/0,9171,869649,00.html.

"Republicans: The Men Who . . ." *Time*, August 8, 1960. http://www.time.com/time/magazine/article/0,9171,869721,00.html.

Ripley, Anthony. "Ohio Girl, 13, Recalls 'Bring Us Together' Placard." *The New York Times*, November 8, 1968.

Schlesinger, Arthur M., Jr. "Inside Conservatism Looking Out." *The New York Times*, October 4, 1959. http://www.nytimes.com/books/00/07/16/specials/buckley-liberalism.html.

Thomas, Evan. "A Heroic Failure." *Newsweek*, August 18, 1996. http://www.thedailybeast.com/newsweek/1996/08/18/a-heroic-failure.html.

"Transcript: Illinois Senate Candidate Barack Obama." *The Washington Post*, July 27, 2004. http://www.washingtonpost.com/wp-dyn/articles/A19751-2004Jul27.html.

Weeks, Edward. "The 1964 Election." *The Atlantic Monthly*, October 1, 1964. http://www.theatlantic.com/magazine/archive/1964/10/the-1964-election/303598/.

Weisman, Jonathan. "GOP Doubts, Fears 'Post-Partisan' Obama." *The Washington Post*, January 7, 2008. http://www.washingtonpost.com/wp-dyn/content/article/2008/01/06/AR2008010602402.html.

Wicker, Tom. "Nixon Makes a New Gain as Republicans Convene; Reagan Avows Candidacy." *The New York Times*, August 5, 1968. http://partners.nytimes.com/library/politics/camp/680806convention-gop-ra.html.

Woodward, Bob, and Carl Bernstein. "Questions Arise About Ford's Pardon of Nixon." *The Spokesman Review*, December 18, 1975. http://news.google.com/newspapers?nid=1314&dat=19751218&id=EfBLAAAAIBAJ&sjid=c-0DAAAAIBAJ&pg=2338,1088253.

Websites

Belin, David W. "The Election of President Ford: Basic Strategy Paper No. 1—November, 1975: Defusing the Reagan Challenge." In Box 7 of the White House Central Files Subject File at the Gerald R. Ford Presidential Library. http://www.ford.utexas.edu/library/exhibits /campaign/005601363-005.pdf.

Buchanan, Patrick J. "Who Killed the New Majority?" http://www .creators.com/opinion/pat-buchanan/who-killed-the-new-majority .html.

Bush, George H. W.. "Address Accepting the Presidential Nomination at the Republican National Convention in New Orleans," August 18, 1988. Online by Gerhard Peters and John T. Woolley, *The American Presidency Project*. http://www.presidency.ucsb.edu/ws/?pid=25955.

Bush, George W. "Address Accepting the Presidential Nomination at the Republican National Convention in Philadelphia," August 3, 2000. Online by Gerhard Peters and John T. Woolley, *The American Presidency Project*. http://www.presidency.ucsb.edu/ws/?pid=25954.

Clinton, William J. "Address Accepting the Presidential Nomination at the Democratic National Convention in New York," July 16, 1992. Online by Gerhard Peters and John T. Woolley, *The American Presidency Project*. http://www.presidency.ucsb.edu/ws/?pid=25958.

Eureka College. "A Young Leader: A Liberal Arts Education at Eureka College." http://reagan.eureka.edu/lead_lessons/leader.htm.

Jones, Jerry H. Jerry H. Jones to Don Rumsfeld and Dick Cheney, September 26, 1975. In Box 25 of the Jerry Jones Files at the Gerald R. Ford Presidential Library. http://www.fordlibrarymuseum.gov /library/exhibits/campaign/016800303-001.pdf.

Neshoba Democrat. "Transcript of Ronald Reagan's 1980 Neshoba County Fair Speech." Last modified November 15, 2007. http://neshoba democrat.com/main.asp?SectionID=2&SubSectionID=297& ArticleID=15599.

Nixon, Richard. "Address Accepting the Presidential Nomination at the Republican National Convention in Chicago," July 28, 1960. Online by Gerhard Peters and John T. Woolley, *The American Presidency Project*. http://www.presidency.ucsb.edu/ws/?pid=25974.

———. "First Inaugural Address," January 20, 1969. http://www.bartleby .com/124/pres58.html.

Presidential History Geeks. "Schlesinger's Essay on the Presidency." Last modified August 14, 2012. http://potus-geeks.livejournal.com /250623.html.

Reagan, Ronald. "Address Before a Joint Session of the Congress Reporting on the State of the Union," January 25, 1984. http://reagan2020 .us/speeches/state_of_the_union_1984.asp.

——. "Labor Day Speech at Liberty State Park, Jersey City, New Jersey," September 1, 1980. http://www.reagan.utexas.edu/archives/reference /9.1.80.html.

Reno, R. R.: "Liberalism and Irritable Mental Gestures." Last modified December 21, 2010. http://www.firstthings.com/blogs/firstthoughts /2010/12/21/liberalism-and-irritable-mental-gestures/.

Republican National Committee. "Republican National Convention Address," August 18, 1992. http://www.c-spanvideo.org/program /31300-1

Sheehy, Gail. "The Inner Quest of Newt Gingrich." http://www.pbs.org /wgbh/pages/frontline/newt/vanityfair1.html.

Shuman, Jim. Jim Shuman to Ron Nessen, November 21, 1975. In Box 138 of the Ron Nessen Papers at the Gerald R. Ford Presidential Library. http://www.fordlibrarymuseum.gov/library/exhibits/campaign /020401482-001.pdf.

"Spiro Theodore Agnew." http://www.americanrhetoric.com/speeches /spiroagnewtvnewscoverage.htm.

White House. "Calvin Coolidge." http://www.whitehouse.gov/about /presidents/calvincoolidge.

About the Author

JOE SCARBOROUGH is the host and creator of *Morning Joe* and was, from 1995 to 2001, a member of the House of Representatives. His previous book, *The Last Best Hope: Restoring Conservatism and America's Promise,* was a *New York Times* bestseller. He was named by *Time* magazine as one of the 100 most influential people in the world.

www.joescarborough.com